70

*THE CENTERS OF CIVILIZATION SERIES*

CAIRO
*City of Art and Commerce*

# CITY OF ART AND COMMERCE

*By Gaston Wiet, translated by Seymour Feiler*

UNIVERSITY OF OKLAHOMA PRESS : NORMAN

LIBRARY OF CONGRESS CATALOG CARD NUMBER: 64–20764

Copyright 1964 by the University of Oklahoma Press, Publishing Division of the University. Composed and printed at Norman, Oklahoma, U.S.A., by the University of Oklahoma Press. First edition.

TO MY CHILDREN,

*Jacques, Denise, and Thérèse*

# Contents

**MAP**

# Foreword

"I enter this peerless
city with joy."—Eugène Fromentin

MY AIM IS TO STUDY the evolution of the Moslem capitals of Egypt, particularly that of Cairo. I shall begin with the Arab conquest, which led to the widespread intermingling of peoples on two continents, and end with the discovery of the route around the Cape of Good Hope, the unprecedented event in the history of world commerce which was to undermine vitally Egypt's active international role.

This book has been written for people of various interests. Writing a volume on Cairo is, under any circumstances, a rash undertaking; it is perhaps the Islamic city which has most intrigued historians; its annals, archaeology, and population have been the subject of many works in all languages. It is, therefore, doubtful that this book, coming after so many others, can be original. Originality would consist in evoking with new words admiration for a civilization whose qualities I do not claim to have discovered. I shall make use of the works of my predecessors, while adding my personal homage. It is impossible not to repeat what they have already said. I have a purpose in mind which is not easy to satisfy. There is much talk today of an integrated study of peoples; in this respect, Orientalists are much behind the times since they even find it difficult to describe the outward behavior of outstanding figures. I should like to give a more precise account of customs and habits and make the past live again, but there are documents which are either missing or have not yet been published and studied.

Cairo has less prestige than the centers of civilization of ancient Egypt, and snobbishness coupled with archaeological finds such as the tomb of Tutankhamen do not help to change things. Yet this city holds a considerable place in the history of art, thanks to a brilliant flourishing of architectural works. There are still characteristic sections of the city which permit our imagination to carry us back to the Middle Ages; the monuments evoke many memories of the past. They bring back to us the events of years gone by. They stand as witnesses that prevent us from belittling and, therefore, falsifying the history of Cairo. There, as elsewhere, the stones sing the glory of the past. We ourselves must look through a hundred tiny streets to find the sweet melancholy of a modest sanctuary. From the northern walls of the Fatimid town to the southern limits of the city, we are accompanied by a harmonious concert that ends in a solemn finale, for we hear a magnificent, proud hymn when our eyes are challenged by the powerful walls of the mosque of Sultan Ḥasan.

When we have climbed to the top of the Citadel, far from the crowds and the street noises, we look down upon "thousands of white, ramshackle buildings, ruins, cemeteries, countless domes and flamboyant minarets." A forest of towers "pointing to the sky" seems to spring up everywhere above a mass of cubes.

Great Cairo, as our European travelers call it, was a political capital from its very creation. As the center of Shī'ism, the city was probably detested, and there was an attempt to limit its influence by a type of sanitary cordon. The city, moreover, had rivals at that time, even though they were only, at one pole, Baghdad, the old center of Islam which had replaced Damascus, and, at the other, Cordova, the center of an unexcelled civilization. Under the Mamlūk sultans Cairo ranks as a universal metropolis, while remaining an Islamic center, and becomes the focal point of the eyes of Europe because of its commercial prosperity.

GASTON WIET

*Neuilly-sur-Seine*
*July 13, 1964*

CAIRO
*City of Art and Commerce*

# 1

## The Early Capitals

THE STUDY OF LATE PREHISTORIC CAIRO poses the problem of the location of the Moslem capitals of Egypt. These were at first important provincial towns before becoming true metropolises.

During the Arab conquest there was first of all Alexandria, which was of no interest to the Arabs who were obliged to maintain their relations with Medina and then with Damascus; after that the Arabs took their orders from Baghdad.

The first city, Fostat, an administrative and military center, grew up around a Babylonian Byzantine fortress. According to a delightful legend, taken as actual fact in the Orient as well as in the Occident, the city grew little by little around the commanding general's tent (*fostat* in Arabic) upon which a wood pigeon had nested its brood. This was believed before the discovery of bilingual papyruses showing the relationship between the Arabic word and the Greek *phossaton*, meaning "entrenched camp." The Moslems, representing the armed forces, did not mingle with the autochthonous population. For reasons of security the Moslems remained together, and, in order for them to be an even more cohesive group at least in Fostat and its suburbs, they were separated according to tribe. Fostat quickly took on the appearance of a city, with its great mosque, which soon had to be enlarged, and its *sūqs* surrounding the sanctuary.

The later development of the city, such as the growth of capitals toward the north, was admirably summarized by an Arab historian: " 'Amr ibn al-'Āṣ entered Egypt at the head of his Moslem armies and founded Fostat, which from that time on became the residence of the governors of the country. Things remained in this state until the end of the Umayyad caliphs. The 'Abbāsid armies built outside of Fostat the section called al-'Askar, where the prefects lived. Ahmed ibn Ṭūlūn later built the palace, the hippodrome, and the section called Qata'i, meaning 'concessions,' near al-'Askar. This new section became the residence of the princes of Ṭūlūn's family. After the extermination of the members of this dynasty, the emirs once again took up residence in al-'Askar until the general of the Fatimid caliph came from the Maghrib and laid the foundations of Cairo. From that time until Saladin destroyed the Fatimid forces, Cairo was the residence of the caliphs of Egypt. When Saladin became the sole master of Egypt, he built the Citadel where his descendants took up residence. The Mamlūks, after having caused the fall of the Ayyūbids and having seized power, followed this example and continued to live in the Citadel."

These various cities were created for military reasons. Since there was no danger from an outside enemy, it would be even more exact to say that the cities were built to protect the chief of state from uprisings. This is far from being an isolated case in the Moslem world.

From a political and artistic point of view, the true history of Moslem Egypt begins with Ibn Ṭūlūn. Finding that the site of al-'Askar lacked security, the new prince wanted a capital, a palace, and a mosque that would perpetuate his memory. Even though the dynasty was of short duration, it is proper to speak of Ṭūlūnid power and art.

Modeling it on Samarra, the Mesopotamian city where he

had grown up, Ibn Ṭūlūn drew up within a given perimeter the plan for the "concessions" to be granted officers, civil servants, and individuals. He also drew the plans for the cathedral mosque and the market places which were to surround it. The rows of markets were to be extensive and were to be separated according to commercial specialty; this same system of separation was used for the various groups of the population. The new city was thus built for the army and the services and commerce indispensable to the daily life of the state. To the east of the city, near the slopes of Muqaṭṭam Mountain, a large area was set aside for riding and horse racing. It was here that military exercises and parades took place.

The reviews of the Ṭūlūnid army on this parade ground were famous throughout the Moslem world of the period, and writers compare it with the *khoṭba* ceremony in Baghdad, which was held in the presence of the caliph. Khumarawayh, Ibn Ṭūlūn's son, enlisted in his personal guard well-built, robust fellows who were chosen for their height and corpulence. He also had a corps of Negroes who passed in review with their heads bound in black turbans and their breasts covered by iron cuirasses over which were worn black tunics. They looked like a black ocean rolling by because of their complexions and their uniforms.

Luxury made its appearance in Egypt with this last prince. He had the palace embellished and enlarged and added an artificial garden with silvered and gilded trees, in Mesopotamian style, which filled the Byzantine ambassadors with admiration. This same garden also contained sweet-smelling plants and trees of the rarest varieties. There was a menagerie where thoroughbred horses, dromedaries, leopards, panthers, elephants, and giraffes were raised. He had tamed a young lion who never left his side. He surrounded himself with a prodigious number of young and beautiful women with whom he seems to have spent almost all the days of his reign.

In one of his palace pavilions, called the Gilded House, he placed before the walls wooden statues one and one-half times life-size representing himself in the company of his favorites and his official female singers. Their heads were encircled with solid gold diadems and turbans set with all types of precious stones, and from their ears hung heavy pendants.

Everything has disappeared, condemned to destruction by the rancor of the ʿAbbāsid caliphate, which did not dare, however, attack the new mosque. This monument conceived by Ibn Ṭūlūn "reflects a harsh, ambitious, proud soul." Here one feels the deepness of the religious sentiment, and one is moved by the magnificent simplicity of the plan, which did not prevent the architect from contrasting the light of the court with the shade of the naves, accentuated by the mass of the pillars. Within the mosque, in the center of an area whose purity is conducive to meditation, one is plunged into an atmosphere of religious contemplation brought about by the harmony of the lines, the mysterious depth of the naves, and the height of the arches, whose severity, already lightened by windows, is further softened by the frieze of rose windows which crowns the top of the walls. The few remaining fragments of decoration on stucco make one think of the artists whose awkwardness is intentional; they have created a linear repertory which future generations can only embellish.

The minaret of the mosque was rebuilt in the thirteenth century but was certainly modeled on the earlier tower which, going back through the prototype of the Samarra mosque, brought to mind the fire altars of Zoroastrianism. Its strange form is explained by a very charming anecdote told by a historian who was the prince's contemporary. Aḥmad ibn Ṭūlūn, who generally maintained a grave attitude during his audiences, one day took a sheet of paper and rolled it around his finger, letting his fingertip show through one end. The spectators looked at each other with a puzzled air, trying to interpret the prince's action. Noticing their astonishment, the emir explained wittily, "I am simply constructing the model of the minaret of my mosque."

The Ṭūlūnids' independence was imitated by the Ikhshidids, whose autonomous regime came just before the arrival of the Fatimids in Egypt. Political facets are of no interest to us here, but it is necessary to point out two cultural facts of primary importance. The traveler and historian Mas'udi lived in Egypt at that time, and he spoke of the economic prosperity of the country in a work which he wrote during his stay there: "All the kingdoms located on the two seas which border the country bring to this commercial center all the most remarkable, the rarest, and the best perfumes, spices, drugs, jewels, and slaves, as well as staples of food and drink, and cloth of all sorts. The merchandise of the entire universe flows to this market."

We should especially remember that the Ikhshidid princes encouraged the talent of Mutanabbi, that giant among Arab poets, whose occasional verse is of vibrant epic inspiration. There is found in his poetry the extraordinary power of the visionary, the uncontested mastery of all the resources of his art, whether they concern rhythm or the happy blending of words. A flatterer by profession, he is saved from baseness by his incomparable genius. It is certainly partly because of

7

him that the Ikhshidids are remembered by posterity with a certain amount of glory.

These two autonomous dynasties had an original attitude toward the Christian minority, probably in order to gain the support of public opinion in facing the Baghdad caliphate. It is sufficient to cite the following description which we owe to Mas'udi and which dates from the year 941: "The evening of Epiphany, the Ikhshidid prince lit on the edge of the isle of Roḍah and on the banks of Fostat a thousand torches in addition to lanterns which illuminated the riverside. There were that night on the banks of the Nile thousands of men, both Moslems and Christians, some in boats and others in the houses on both banks of the Nile which were closest to the river. Nothing that could be put on display was neglected: food, drink, clothing, gold and silver utensils, jewels, amusements, music, and excellent meals. It was the most beautiful and most pleasurable night that was ever seen in Fostat. The streets were not closed that night. Most of the participants dived into the Nile; they claimed that this prevented illness and was a talisman against disease."

Moslem political regimes are centralized. The success of a double task which devolved upon the new masters, Islamization and Arabization, can, therefore, be attributed to the capital of Egypt, under the directives of the caliphate, of course.

William Marçais has clearly exposed the attitude of the early Moslems on the problems of education: "Educational objectives, in Moslem society, are concerned, or even confused, with the desire to permit each man to carry out his religious duties, to strengthen the faith of the believers, and to convert the nonbelievers. Promoting among their subjects the diffusion of useful knowledge to all those who profess Islam is a strict duty of those who govern."

A quick summary of the steps leading to the conversion of the Copts to Islam shows that the Christians had become a minority in the ninth century, two hundred years after the Arab conquest; this was, then, a rapid triumph. In Fostat—and that is what interests us particularly—Arabization was just as fast. In less than three centuries, Arabic almost totally eliminated its rival language, Coptic. The most important document on this subject is Severus of Ashmunain's preface to his *History of the Patriarchs of Alexandria*, written at the end of the tenth century. He wrote: "I have solicited the aid of Christians who translated for me what they had read in Coptic, in Greek, and in the Arabic language which has spread to such a point in Egypt today that most of the inhabitants do not know Greek or Coptic."

From the very first, the mosque was the center of education. This was natural since education was concerned with training experts in the Koran and the Ḥadith. This meant learning the holy texts by heart and repeating them without any lapses of memory or grammatical errors. It was in this way that one could become a good Moslem and a serious and zealous missionary. The professor of Koranic studies was indispensable in all mosques. According to Ibn Jubayr, "the instruction in the Koran given to young boys in all the countries of the Orient is reduced to sing-song recitation. They are taught to write through poems and other texts, in order to protect the Lord's Book from the children's carelessness in writing and from erasures. Instruction in the chanting of the Koran is kept separate from lessons in writing."

A type of private instruction existed in that money was

set aside to pay any man who decided to lecture as he sat in the mosque and leaned against one of the pillars. Charitable organizations paid for the support of orphans who were considered capable of benefiting from religious instruction. From the seventh century on, distinguished traditionalists began to make their appearance in Fostat. These venerable sages were assisted by popular preachers of no mean merit, who drew their inspiration from earlier satires.

Thus, the educational formula appealed especially to memory. At the beginning, writing played a minor role, and this important fact would have a decisive influence for centuries on scholastic discipline. This was the method used by reciters and readers of the Koran from earliest times. In any event, the child learned to read and write, which was no mean feat. The student, then, was to learn the Koran by heart and recite it while chanting according to very definite rules.

The Koran was, therefore, the essential base of the instruction and education of a Moslem. At first the pupils read the entire text. Then they were asked to memorize as much of it as they could. After a grammatical analysis of all the text, the teachers asked the students to transcribe it in its traditional form. During this process, the teachers clearly interpreted the text. Memorizing the Koran was not only an indication of culture, but it also marked the man of learning among his contemporaries. Historians have been careful to conserve for posterity the names of those who devoted themselves to this exercise of memory.

It is equally certain that another aim of education was the very early transmission of the Ḥadith. The program was composed of two sections: the obligatory one was concerned with the teaching of the Koran, religious instruction, reading, and writing; the optional one included pre-Islamic history, the history of the Prophet and his companions, poetry, grammar, composition, vocabulary, arithmetic, and calligraphy. Mnemonic techniques, of course, were numerous; no other literature is as rich in didactic poetry offering the student treatises on astronomy, mathematics, history, and especially law. It is not until the eighth century and the invention of paper that there "is a diminishing of the prejudice according to which the oral transmission of knowledge was alone legitimate."

The treatises of some rigorists did not permit primary education in the mosques, for the children might dirty the walls. They suggest that classes be held in shops located on the streets or on the outskirts of the market places. Most classes, except those which met outdoors, were held in very small meeting places. We can give a picture of what the medieval primary school must have been like, according to modern descriptions. All the pupils gather in one meeting place and recite and learn their assigned lessons aloud. We can imagine the noise that was heard in the classroom; in order to stand it, the teachers must have been quite accustomed to it. In addition to chanting as they recited or read their lessons, as was done in all countries, the children also rocked the upper parts of their bodies back and forth. This perpetual movement, joined with the discordant sound of all those voices, made for a strange sight in Arab schools. The children who did not do their assignments or who were disrespectful to their teachers were severely punished. The guilty pupil was placed on his back on the ground. An assistant held up his legs so that the sheik could fit the pupil's feet into a *falaqa*, similar to stocks, used from the Byzantine period to contemporary times. The sheik then beat the victim's feet with fine palm branches. The profession of schoolmaster was held in contempt; an expression of the time was: "Stupider than a schoolmaster." This attitude is not peculiar to Arab civilization.

More advanced instruction was given in the mosques. The placing of the students in a circle (*halqa* in Arabic) around the teacher, who sat leaning against a column or pillar of the mosque, presents a familiar picture which is seen to this very day. In primary schools, in mosque classes, or even later in the madrasahs, the students were seated on mats placed on the ground. The teachers in schools of higher education had a great deal of difficulty maintaining discipline in their courses. There was a constant flow of questions from students, who did not hesitate to ask for explanations. Some of the teachers complained bitterly about this. This modern-day sketch can be applied to classrooms of all periods: "One can see the turban of the teacher who is squatting on his sheepskin. In front of his bare feet, there are a pair of babouches and a towel. Around his column, there are three rows of auditors, resembling the strands of a necklace. They, too, are barefoot and have carefully placed their babouches in front of them, like a display of fruit."

It was proper for the student, while receiving his religious instruction, to learn Arabic thoroughly so that he could understand correctly the Holy Book. This instruction in language could not be carried out without intensive study of ancient poetry.

We can now understand the enthusiasm of the Persian traveler, Naṣir-i-Khūsrau, in the middle of the eleventh century, who describes for us the result of the educational mission of the great mosque of Fostat: "In the court, there are always teachers and readers of the Koran. This is the meeting place of the inhabitants of this great city; here one never sees a gathering of less than five thousand people, students, foreigners, and public scribes who draw up bills of exchange, contracts, and other papers."

At the time when these lines were written, Shī'ism was the official doctrine of the Egyptian state. If we remember that Alexandria was from the early centuries of the Christian era an active center of heresy, it becomes important for us to note that, from the time of the arrival of the Arabs, the country had almost completely avoided the religious and political dissensions which tore apart Mesopotamia, Persia, and North Africa. Certainly some isolated individuals must have defended heterodox theses, but Egypt, remaining outside the Kharijite struggles and all their subdivisions, was quite indifferent to the problems of determinism and free will, and almost completely side-stepped the Mutazilite persecutions.

It is perhaps of some use, in this respect, to point out that the great sage of Islam, al-Shāfi'ī, spent the last years of his life in Fostat, where he is buried. The role that he played in elaborating religious law is so important that it cannot be exaggerated, for he was truly the founder of methodology in the field of religious legislation. He scientifically created a coherent doctrine. It should be recalled that there were two tendencies. The traditionalists, who can be called members of the historical school, basing their ideas on the respect due Mohammed, claimed to establish moral law almost completely on tradition, without entirely forbidding analogy and personal opinion when necessary. The partisans of the personal point of view, who can be called members of the rational school—with some reservation—started out, too, with great respect for tradition, but because they felt that there was a scarcity of authentic material, they opened the door to individual common sense.

Shāfiʿī's effort was conciliatory. We owe to him the definition and the rigorous application of the four sources of law, which are the Koran, tradition, consensus of the community, and analogy. His originality consists in extending consensus to the entire communal group. This gave legal force to unanimously recognized usage. This is then the proclamation of the infallibility of the community, which the Shafiʿites define as the unanimous accord of the sages of a given period.

Whatever the case may be, before the founding of Cairo, Fostat was certainly not a center of literary and theological activity which could be compared in importance and fame with cities such as Baghdad, Basra, or Al Kūfa.

We shall finish this period by citing a rather elusive historical figure, Dhul-Nūn, claimed by mystics, alchemists, and cabalists. Certain fragments of his works—maxims, parables, anecdotes—are mystic. He has left this definition of the divinity of God: "God is the opposite of everything you imagine."

# 2

# Fatimid Cairo

THE CAPITAL OF Ibn Ṭūlūn never went beyond the status of a palatine city. This fact influenced somewhat the devastating rage of the 'Abbāsid general who was in command at the time of the fall of the dynasty. Cairo was to enjoy more lasting glory.

Even before the Fatimids, Egypt's masters had already begun to move toward the north. Indeed, the last of the Ikhshidids had created the Kafur park at some distance from the al-'Askar and Fostat settlement. This vast garden, a part of which was still kept up by the Fatimids,was built on the same level as the al-Aqmar mosque and was bordered by the Cairo Canal. The sovereigns of Cairo reached this part, which became their private garden, through underground passages.

Cairo was a new city, created where nothing had existed before, on a site expressly chosen beforehand, situated on a sandy plain. The first night after arriving in Fostat, the general in charge of the Fatimid armies, Jauhar, following the plans drawn up by the caliph himself in North Africa, had the walls of Cairo traced north of the old capital and had the foundations of the royal palace laid. Long before, for the founding of Baghdad, the most competent specialists had determined when the stars would be most favorable for such an undertaking. Similar precautions were taken for the building of Cairo.

"Having decided to build his capital, Jauhar called his

astrologers and told them of his desire to found a city for his army. He ordered them to choose the best horoscope for the founding of the capital so that the descendants of the caliphs would never be dispossessed from the city. They then chose a horoscope for the laying of the foundations and the digging of the trenches for the walls. Along the entire length of the ramparts, they set up wooden posts which were tied together, two by two, by cords from which they hung small bells. They said to the workmen, 'When the bells ring, throw the mortar and the stones, which you have close at hand, along the line of the fortifications.' They then remained ready to act at the propitious moment. Suddenly a crow lit on one of the cables and all the bells rang. Believing that the astrologers had rung them, the workmen moved the mortar and the stones that they had near at hand and set to work. The astrologers cried out, 'Qahir, the planet Mars, is in the ascendant!' They went on with their work, and their plans were undone. Mars was in the ascendant at the beginning of the laying of the foundations and dominated the sphere. That is why they gave the city the name *Qahira*, the Martian."

The city of Cairo was founded on July 6, 969, and quarters were assigned to the various troops six months later. The new city extended from the southern minaret of al-Ḥakim mosque to Zuweila gate; in the east the limits were the same as those of modern Cairo, but toward the west they did not go beyond the canal. The royal palace was built at the same time as the city; its western façade ran from the al-Aqmar mosque to the al-Malik al-Ṣālih Ayyūb school. The first stone of the al-Azhar mosque was laid on April 4, 970, and the building was finished on June 22, 972.

Thus a city was born, a city which was to be, because of its heterodox tendencies, the object of Sunnite bitterness. As a matter of fact, the coming to power of the Fatimids in Egypt caused an unusual upheaval. From the time of their seizure of North Africa, they became the rivals of the Baghdad 'Abbāsid. And a short time later, in 929, the Umayyad prince of Cordova, following the lead of the Fatimids themselves by appealing to public opinion, considered it proper for him to assume the title of caliph, too. He judged, in his message to the people, "that any further neglect of what was his due would constitute the loss of a right and the renunciation of a title to which he had legitimate claim." This could truly be called the period of the Great Schism because of the multiplication of caliphates. The term is a just one, for if the caliphs of Baghdad and Cordova maintain the fiction of being approved by a badly defined electoral elite, the Fatimid caliph, the imam, lays claim to a special mission. His nomination does not depend upon such ordinary things as popular decision. He is designated by his sacred ancestry, and he himself is faultless.

Housing was built for the military men and their families, and special commercial shops were set up for their use. "As the ramparts were going up and the foundations of the palaces and the great al-Azhar mosque were rising, Jauhar's soldiers were building homes, and the camp was becoming a city. When the land within the walls had been assigned to the various army units, each one of them built up an area to which it gave its name or the name of its commander. Cairo was at that time divided almost equally in two by a large boulevard running parallel to the canal, which flowed westward. The streets of the main sections of the city opened out on both sides of the boulevard."

To the west of the canal there were gardens that stretched to the banks of the Nile. Here there was frequently a large crowd of idlers and strollers seeking amusement and entertainment. When the waters of the Nile rose to their highest point, the caliph would go to one of the pavilions set up on the plain, and there was a great deal of popular merriment.

In this palatine and military city, street care was no great problem. Goatskin bottles of water transported by camel or mule had to be covered in order not to splash passers-by. In addition, each shopkeeper had to have in front of his establishment a jar full of water with which to help fight fires. An ordinance of the caliph Ḥakim is of some interest. The order was given throughout the city that shops, doorways, squares, thoroughfares, and dead-end streets were to be lit up. The people began to exaggerate their use of lights in the streets and alleys. The indoor and outdoor markets in Cairo and Old Cairo kept their lights burning all night and had crowds of customers. Considerable amounts of money were spent on eating and drinking parties and concerts. Caliph Ḥakim, whose eccentricity needs no further demonstration, was soon scandalized and ordered a strict curfew.

A Persian traveler who spent some time in Cairo was full of praise: "Cairo is a great city with which few cities can be compared. I have figured that there are no fewer than twenty-thousand shops, all belonging to the sovereign. Caravansaries, baths, and other public buildings are so numerous that they would be difficult to count. All of these buildings are the property of the caliph, for no one can own houses unless he has had them built for himself. I have been told that there are in Cairo and in Old Cairo twenty-thousand houses belonging to the caliph, all of which are rented. Rent is collected once a month. The tenant may rent a house or move out of it, as he pleases, without any further obligation.

"The city is not enclosed by a fortified wall. The buildings and the houses are so tall that they are higher than the ramparts. Each palace, each house can be considered a citadel. Most of the houses are five or six storeys high. The houses are separated from each other by orchards and gardens and are sprinkled with well-water. They are built with such care and luxury that you would think they were made of precious stones and not of plaster, bricks, and ordinary stones. All the houses are isolated so that the trees of one do not encroach upon the walls of another.

"Drinking water is furnished by the Nile, and water-carriers bring it to the city on camel back. The camels which carry goatskin bottles of water to Cairo number, I am told, fifty-two thousand. Water-carriers, who bear on their backs copper vases or small goatskin bottles, go into the narrow streets where camels cannot pass.

"The Caliph's palace rises in the middle of the city of Cairo; the approaches to it are free of all construction, and there are no buildings adjoining it. There is a clearing completely around it. Every night one thousand men—five hundred horsemen and five hundred foot-soldiers—are assigned to guard the palace."

A solemn ceremony was connected with the nightly protection of the palace. After muezzin had announced the time for the last evening prayer and an imam had recited it, an emir advanced to the doorstep of the palace. At the end of the prayer, he gave the order to the band of drummers and trumpeters to play, and other instruments too played beautiful pieces of music for about an hour. Then an officer, specially charged with this duty, left the palace, brandished a lance, threw it first into the ground at the threshold, then snatched it up, closed the door, and marched around the palace seven times. After having finished his rounds, he posted the night sentinels and the pages of the guard. A chain was placed across the narrowest part of the square called "Between the Two Palaces." From that moment on, all traffic ceased on the square until a fanfare announced dawn. The chain was then removed and traffic resumed.

Our Iranian guide continues: "Seen from outside the city, the palace is taken for a mountain because of the massiveness and the height of its buildings; but from within the city it cannot be seen because its surrounding walls are very high. The palace consists of twelve pavilions. Ten gates lead to the enclosed section. Some of them are on ground level, others are underground. There is a door above ground which closes on a subterranean passage. The caliph rides his horse through this passage in order to get to another palace. The vault of this passage running from one palace to the other is of solid construction. The walls of the palaces are so well put together that they appear to be hewn out of a single block."

Let us enter the palace with our guide, Naṣir-i-Khūsrau: "I saw a series of buildings, terraces, and rooms. There were twelve adjoining pavilions, all of them square in shape. Upon entering, one finds each to be even more beautiful than the last. There was a throne in one of them which took up the entire width of the room. Three of its sides were made of gold on which were hunting scenes, depicting riders racing their horses, and other subjects; there were also inscriptions written in beautiful characters. The rugs and hangings were of Greek satin and moire woven precisely to fit the spot where they were to be placed. A balustrade of golden latticework surrounded the throne, whose beauty defies all description. Behind the throne, there were steps of silver. I saw a tree, which looked like an orange tree, whose branches, leaves, and fruit were made of sugar. A thousand statuettes and figurines also made of sugar were placed there."

A report, written by William of Tyre, of the visit of Frankish ambassadors to Cairo in 1167 is worthy of our attention. The envoys, guided by the vizier Shāwar in person, were first taken to a very beautiful, richly decorated palace. There a large number of guards accompanied them, walking on ahead with bared swords. Led through long, narrow, vaulted passages, where they could see nothing because of the complete darkness, the envoys finding themselves once again in the light saw a series of doors. Numerous guards stationed at each door rose immediately at the approach of Shāwar and saluted him respectfully. The envoys then came into an outdoor court which was surrounded by magnificent colonnaded porticoes. The court was completely paved with marble of various colors, set off with gold of extraordinary richness. The rafters and beams were all covered with gold. It was so beautiful, so pleasant to behold, that the most pre-occupied person would have stopped to stare. Through gold and silver pipes, a centrally located fountain furnished magnificently clear water to canals and pools which were paved with marble. Here and there flitted an infinite variety of birds of the rarest colors and of the most beautiful species, which had come from all parts of the Orient. Everyone who saw them was amazed and said that a rejoicing nature had created them. Depending upon their habits, some of these birds stayed close to the fountains while others remained at a distance. Each bird was fed what best suited it. The first guards who had escorted the Frankish warriors left them at this point. They were immediately replaced by more important people, who were on intimate terms with the caliph. These new guides led the envoys through even more beautiful courts and through a garden which was so rich and delightful that the first one seemed insignificant. There they saw a menagerie of quadrupeds which were so strange that anyone telling of them would be accused of lying and which no artist could paint even in a dream. After having gone through many more doors and along many more walks and seeing new things which dazzled them even more greatly, they finally arrived at the Great Palace, the residence of the caliph. This was even more sumptuous than anything they had seen up to that point. The courts teemed with armed Saracen warriors dressed in sparkling gold and silver armor, who seemed to be proud of the treasures they guarded. The Frankish chiefs were shown into a vast room which was separated in two, from one wall to the other, by a curtain strewn with figures of animals, birds, and people and flaming with rubies, emeralds, and a thousand precious stones. There was no one in this room. Nevertheless, as soon as Shāwar had entered, he prostrated himself as though in worship, arose, prostrated himself again, and laid down the sword which usually hung from his neck. A third time he prostrated himself and remained in a position of humblest worship. Then suddenly, with the rapidity of a bolt of lightning, cords raised like a veil the large gold and silk tapestry which hid the front of the room, and the child caliph appeared before the dazzled eyes of the Latin envoys. The face of this mysterious prince was completely covered by a veil. He was seated on a golden throne set with gems and precious stones.

Let us stop for a while and examine the wood carvings that come from these palaces. These justly famous carvings offer scenes that are divided into rather unexpected sequences: hunting, music sessions, dances, drinking bouts. The

artists who thought up these scenes did not completely abandon their need for balance and methodical planning. Some
of the works even portray groups of animals confronting each
other, some frozen in beautifully calm positions; but most
of them are treated with a keen sense of movement. The
general rhythm is constant, with the alternating of little
multiple lobed figures with oblong hexagons. This contrast
of distribution goes along with the harmony of the forms
which are repeated symmetrically on the right and the left
of a central scene. The decoration is carried out on two
planes: little people, animals, and birds stand out against a
background of scrolls and three-lobed leaves, which are of
less salient relief. Each one of the scenes is doubly isolated
by its frame and by the animals which flank it. Diversity adds
to their charm. When taken all together, they represent the
various aspects of the daily life of the monarch. These wood-
carvings, with their studied sobriety, are masterpieces in
the art of silhouette. The perfect reproduction of folds in
cloth, for example, was not conceivable. What should be
stressed is the simplicity of procedure used by these sculptors
to evoke dance steps of intense vivacity. The artists who did
these carvings created pictures full of exuberance and of an
almost sensual beauty. The artistic conceptions are ardent
and revolutionary.

These descriptions are eloquent enough to offer an appre-
ciation of the luxury in which the Fatimid caliphs lived.
Their palaces contained many storerooms which were both
warehouses and places to keep curiosities. Arab writers have
helpfully listed the following: the clothing room in which
were stored the linens and clothes that the caliph, with great
detriment to the state budget, distributed profusely to his
high-ranking employees; the room in which were kept col-

lections of precious pearls and stones, various objects of rock crystal and porcelain, mirrors, chess sets with ebony, ivory, silver, and gold pawns, golden table-service, as well as a prodigious quantity of the rarest perfumes; the tapestry room containing rugs and cloth embroidered with gold and silver figures of all sorts of animals, including elephants and other quadrupeds, birds, and men, and also containing immense tents used on trips—in short, all the furnishings belonging to the crown; the armory where were found weapons of all sorts—swords, lances, cuirasses, helmets, caparisons, bows, arrows, and javelins; the saddle and harness room; a store-room for beverages; a fabulous room for spices, with the greatest variety of condiments, wax, honey, refined sugar, sugar candy, sesame oil, and olive oil; the banner room, which held flags and gold and silver canes and which also served as a jail for officers and important persons; and finally the vast dessert room where pastries and sweets were prepared.

The palaces and the objects of art formed an appropriate background for the joyous devil-may-care attitude which was prevalent in Cairo. We know in detail the order of the holidays celebrated by the Fatimid dynasty, holidays which were pretexts for the distribution of food and money to the poor and banquets and bonuses for the state employees. This recurring largess was extremely frequent, for joined to the ceremonies of Sunnite Islamism, recognized by the Fatimids, were the Shī'ite celebrations, Christian holidays, and days of rejoicing firmly established by the secular traditions of the country—the noisy manifestations when the Nile rose, for example.

The Fatimids were not the first ones in Egypt to honor Christian holidays with their presence. Yet, with some very few exceptions, the favor enjoyed by the Christians grew with the arrival of the Fatimids. It should not be forgotten that commerce and agriculture were almost exclusively in Christian hands. One can understand, too, that the Ismailian doctrines propagated in Egypt alienated a large part of the Moslem masses. Very naturally practicing a policy of balances, the Fatimid ministers tried to find among the Christians the popularity which they had lost elsewhere. It should finally be added that there were many Christians in administrative positions.

We have a budget from the year 1123, which lists the following: Moslem and local holidays, expenses for royal retinues, receptions for ambassadors, and subsidies for poets. We are rather well informed on all the details of the ceremonies of this period of the twelfth century, the lavish court banquets, and the caliph's grants.

According to established custom, the sovereign offered two feasts a year, at the time of the canonical holidays. He invited both the high-ranking officials and the people. The meals to which he invited the court personalities were held in his presence; those given to the people were served in public buildings. The sovereign's private kitchens were outside the palace; fifty servants were employed in them at all times. An underground passage led from the palace to the kitchens. We are informed of a special refinement: every day fourteen camels carried snow coming from Lebanon to the sovereign's larders. Most of the important officers and dignitaries received fixed rations of this snow. Some was also given to townspeople upon demand to help the sick.

These rulers, avidly fond of pomp and ceremony, are no longer remembered for their mad desire to dominate the world. They were the builders of a refined civilization. Because of their love for luxury in all its forms—buildings which they have left us, works of art with which they surrounded themselves, and sumptuous materials for their clothing and palace furnishings—the caliphs of Egypt proved that they were not barbarians, but rather beings of delicate character with noble and productive minds.

Cairo at first had a wall made of brick. It was only at the end of the eleventh century that minister Badr al-Jamāli replaced this insignificant wall with strong, solid ramparts of hewn stone. They give evidence of a perfect technique quite different from that used in building the earlier mosques. The three monumental gates which have lasted, Bāb Zuweila to the south, Bāb al-Naṣr and Bāb al-Futūḥ to the north, were built, if we are to believe the Arab writers, by three brothers who came from Upper Mesopotamia. They resemble Roman gates, especially Bāb al-Naṣr with its salient squares of magnificent stone, its molding, and its modillions. It was bounded on the west by a double road for the rounds of the guards. The interior was completely covered and furnished with lateral openings, wide embrasures through which archers could keep watch or shoot their arrows. There are semicircular vaults, cradle-vaults, vaults with multiple moldings, and cupolas on pendentives; these loopholes are finished with a stone elegantly hewn in the shape of the frustum of a cone. On the first floor above the two sections of the gate there is an archers' room provided with machicolations.

Those who traveled during past centuries marveled at these magnificent works. One of these voyagers says, in speaking of Bāb al-Futūḥ, that he has "never seen anything so beautiful, so ancient, or so complete. Two towers form the principal decoration of this gate. These towers are not en-

tirely round; they are almost oval in shape. The workmanship is so nearly perfect, that the towers seem to be made of
a single stone."

The voice of these walls has remained silent. No one
watching behind the crenels has ever announced the presence
of an enemy; the portcullises have never been used; boiling
oil and molten lead have never been poured on the heads of
attackers. The walls never even frightened the poor, who
must very soon have built their shacks up against them.

Of the entire Fatimid city there remain only the vestiges
of the main street, running north and south, several alleys,
and such magnificent landmarks as the al-Azhar, the al-
Aqmar, and the caliph al-Ḥakim mosques.

The crowning glory of the Fatimid dynasty is the al-Azhar
mosque, almost isolated from the world at present, turning
its back on the reality of daily life. It is a beehive of work
and piety. Since the building had to be enlarged with time,
it has become a sort of museum of Moslem forms of architecture and decoration. It is an immense assemblage of arches
and columns of the most diverse styles. The founder could
not have forseen the gigantic developments which were to
upset the original plan and destroy the unity of style. The
monument is, therefore, a composite which must be accepted
as such. Destined to be a religious school, a great seminary,
it is the result of the combined effort of several generations of
princes who wished to enlarge and enrich it.

Originally, it was the classical type of Mosque with porticoes. The one notable modification, imported from North
Africa, was the greater width given to the central choir
nave, making it a sort of triumphal aisle. Some people have
claimed to see in this plan the temple of a nomad race. There
is a better explanation. The plan goes well with a simple

27

dogma and an uncomplicated cult. This is even more striking in Egypt, for formerly in the temples of antiquity there
was a sanctum sanctorum in an obscure retreat where only
the kings and rare initiates had the right to enter and con-
template the majesty of the god. Certain impressive vaults
of our Western forests make us think of the giant naves of a
cathedral; in the same way, we notice a relationship between
the atmosphere of a columned mosque and that of a palm
grove, whose arrangement is sometimes very symmetrical.
Like the mosque, the palm grove is "a forest without mystery,
and the severe rigidity of its tree trunks passes across space
without obscuring it." Another comparison between church
and mosque is evident. The church reaches toward the sky
with the thrust of the nave, its towers, its bell turrets, and
its steeples. Michelet saw the flying buttresses as crutches
which help the church in its ascent. The mosque sprawls out,
fixed to the earth, like a symbol of serenity, fidelity, and
quiet courage, lacking that drama of humility and hope
which is played in the church.

The Fatimids also created a new sanctuary, a commemo-
rative monument erected over the true or supposed tombs
of the principal 'Alids worthy of special devotion. They
favored rendering homage to the suffering faith, to the
'Alid martyrs. It is thus that the cult of the saints spread very
rapidly. Not only were the pious figures of the golden legend
of Islam included, but so were the patriarchs of the Old
Testament. From the immediately following period on, we
have pilgrimage guides containing very precise lists of the
names of the venerated saints. The head of Ḥusain, the
martyr of Karbala, the son of Caliph 'Ali, was brought to
Cairo, as was the head of Zain al-'Ābidīn. Ibn Jubayr lists the
shrines visited in his time. Despite the Sunnite revival, the

Shī'ite mausoleums remained the object of popular fervor. The city of Cairo thus owes most of its guardian saints to a Shī'ite government.

Even though we may admire the civilization of the Fatimids, we must not be fooled by the monuments and the objects of art which they certainly sponsored. We must, of necessity, examine letters and science and present a succinct cultural geography of the Moslem world. In Islam's eastern domain, under the Samanid family, a pleiad of writers, among whom are Rudaki and the historian Bal'ami, lends brilliance to the Persian language for the first time. The Ḥamanids of Aleppo protect the philosopher Fārābi, the poet Mutanabbi, and his emulator Abu Firas. In Persia, Ḥamadhāni and Ḥariri wrote the famous *Sessions*, playlets full of picaresque humor, while in Syria the blind poet Abul 'Ala al-Ma'arri raised his voice in pessimism and despair. It should not be forgotten that the eleventh century is dominated by literary giants such as Firdausi, the creator of the Iranian epic, and the two greatest scholars of their time, Avicenna and Biruni. The Fatimid dynasty disappeared in 1171 without making any valuable contribution to letters or science. It offered no one to rival Ghazāli and 'Omar al-Khayyām in the East or Avenzoar and Averroës in Spain in the West.

In earlier times Mesopotamia's best scholars of the Arabic language, through appropriate translations, had gathered up the heritage of the wisdom of antiquity. At the time when the Fatimids took over the Egyptian throne, the great efforts of the translators were already finished and scientific vocabulary was perfected. They, therefore, turned their attention to making of the capital of Egypt, already the political rival of Baghdad and Cordova, a cultural center which, they thought, would surpass its predecessors. Let us see how they went about this.

Ibn Killis, a former Jew converted to Islam with great ostentation, was the founder of higher theological education in the al-Azhar mosque in 988. Thirty-five jurists were appointed to give courses there.

Modeling itself on Mesopotamian institutions, except for doctrine which remained Shī'ite, it became a type of "universal academy in which were taught, in addition to the truly Moslem courses of study, the disciplines inherited from antiquity, such as mathematics, astronomy, surveying, physical and natural sciences, medicine, grammar, poetry, the arts, and the various branches of philosophy."

Research was made possible by a library set up by the caliphate in the Great Palace. This library consisted of forty rooms containing an extraordinary number of books on a great variety of subjects. It was the largest one in Moslem territory at that time and could be considered one of the wonders of the world. The library contained a great number of closets, lined up around each room and separated by partitions in each of which was a solid door closed by locks and bolts. There were 100,000 bound or stitched volumes on religious law according to the various sects; collections on tradition; treatises on grammar, astronomy, and alchemy; chronicles; and personal histories of a great number of princes. There were several copies of each book. A sheet of paper pasted to the door of each closet listed the manuscripts contained in it.

The Korans were kept separate in a special room; these were copied by hand by the most famous calligraphers. The collection consisted of 2,400 copies of the greatest beauty, decorated with gold, silver, and other ornaments.

This priceless collection disappeared in the most deplorable manner. The beautiful manuscripts were disposed of so that the troops could be paid. Those books that still remained at the time of the fall of the dynasty were auctioned off and dispersed.

Aside from this purely scholarly undertaking, the Fatimids had provided for catechistic instruction in one of the palace rooms. Shī'ite doctrine was taught, and, we imagine, attendance at these courses was obligatory for certain groups of individuals. Private sessions were even held for women.

An Arab historian provides this detailed information: "On Saturday, March 24, 1005, the house called the House of Knowledge was opened in Cairo. Jurisconsults were assigned to it, and books were brought from the palace libraries. Everyone was free to enter and to read or copy anything he desired. This house was carefully decorated and furnished with rugs and curtains. Curators and employees were assigned to assure service. Then lecturers, astronomers, grammarians, and physicians were hired. The library that Caliph al-Ḥakim had supplied contained works on various subjects, books copied by the hand of the most famous calligraphers. This formed the greatest collection that any prince had ever assembled. All these manuscripts were at the disposition of those who wanted to read or examine them. Through his laudable and unprecedented generosity, al-Ḥakim granted a yearly salary to the jurisconsults and all the others who were attached to this establishment. Everyone was admitted without distinction. Some came to read the books, others to make copies, and still others to listen to the lectures of the different teachers. Paper, ink, and pens were provided at need. In the year 1013, al-Ḥakim summoned several mathematicians, logicians, jurisconsults, and physicians who were attached to the House of Knowledge. Each category of scholars was called separately to confer in the presence of the caliph, who plied them with gifts and had them dressed in robes of honor."

As we have seen, no great name stands out among the poets or among writers of incontestable literary merit. We should not be taken in by the "men of letters, scholars, and numerous poets supported by the caliph" of whom Naṣir-i-Khūsrau speaks.

The sciences are more favored, for several scholars of great standing represent Egypt in this outburst of scientific activity engaged in, with much rivalry, by all the centers of the Moslem world.

Ibn Yūnus was one of the greatest astronomers ever to have written in the Arabic language. The observatory on the hill overlooking Cairo was the site where he carried on his research, the result of which was set down in the Ḥakimid Tables, dedicated to Caliph al-Ḥakim. He was the first to discover a formula in the trigonometry of the sphere, which, before the discovery of logarithms, was of great use to astronomers, since it substituted addition for the complicated multiplication of trigonometric functions expressed in sexagesimal fractions. He displayed great ability in solving several problems in spherical astronomy by resorting to the orthogonal projection of the celestial orb on the horizon and on the meridian plane.

Ibn al-Haitham, called Alhazen in medieval Europe, who lived in the same period, became a first-rate scholar in the history of science. His productivity was equaled only by the diversity of his interests, since he wrote about balance, the structure of the world, the distance of the Milky Way, rainbows, the determination of the *qiblah*—the direction of

Mecca from any given city—music, spherical and parabolic mirrors, sunlight, and magic squares. He was called from Mesopotamia to Egypt to solve a practical problem at which he failed. It concerned the utilization of the waters of the Nile, regardless of their level, for the purposes of irrigation. Indeed, to accomplish this, it would have been necessary to undertake the practical application of science in Egypt and to write treatises concerning elevating machines. Ibn al-Haitham's most original work was his *Treatise on Optics*, which, when it appeared, filled a gap in Arab science. There was available a translation of Euclid's work on optics, for which the philosopher Kindi had written a commentary. Ibn al-Haitham's *Optics* had a decisive influence on European physicists. It is in his work that the camera obscura is described for the first time.

'Ammar ibn 'Ali, the most original oculist of the Arab world, settled in Egypt after having traveled in the Orient for a long time. He dedicated to Caliph al-Ḥakim his work on the diseases of the eye. If he was not the inventor of the resorption technique in cataract operations, he did perfect the suction procedure, in which a hollow needle was used. This practice was considered dangerous and ineffectual.

Ibn Riḍwan, Caliph al-Ḥakim's physician, left a curious work on climatology. He is known particularly because of his controversy with his colleague from northern Syria, the Christian Ibn Buṭlan. Their dispute centered on the degree to which chicks and goslings are warm natured. The argument became more serious when the two scholars, through professional pride, as often happens in such cases, began to use sarcasm. Ibn Buṭlan especially maintained that oral instruction was indispensable in training physicians, while self-taught Ibn Riḍwan claimed that all necessary information could be found in books. Both men kept in view the notion of scientific progress defined in the preceding century by the philosopher and physician al-Razi, whom we call Rhazes. These two representatives of free discussion in the Arab world should be honored. Soon the madrasah, the religious school and the only school, was to limit Moslem thought to a far lower level. This, in the Near East, was the last spurt of philosophical and, especially, scientific studies, and of observations of natural and firmamental phenomena, under the influence of Shī'ite thought.

\* \* \*

The seven years of famine during the reign of Mustanṣir seem to have harmed Fostat rather than Cairo. The first of these cities lost its inhabitants, and its houses soon fell into ruin. Cairo, too, had certainly been affected, and some sections of the city were deserted. Fostat became a depopulated ruin crumbling behind its framework. Many property owners died without heirs. The all-powerful minister Badr al-Jamāli, therefore ordered all those who could to build in Cairo and immediately to its south. They were to use materials taken from the debris of Fostat. This advice, or rather this order, was carried out, and many persons used this material to build homes in Cairo.

It was later, under the reign of Caliph 'Āmir, that buildings were constantly being erected between Cairo and Fostat. Government employees went home from their work in Cairo to Old Cairo through continuously bustling streets illuminated by lamps. The vizier Ma'mun renewed the order forbidding property owners in this zone to build or to sell their lands to purchasers, who were obliged to build, without diverting to use these materials. If the order was not obeyed, the owners would forfeit to the state their title to the land.

This resulted in a certain amount of renewed prosperity for the region between Bāb Zuweila and the Sayyida Nafisa shrine.

In addition, the re-establishment of army corps, undertaken by Badr al-Jamāli, caused a housing problem. The new units could not be quartered within the limits of the city itself. They were housed outside the ramparts, toward the south, and markets were set up for their daily needs. In these markets there were cloth merchants, druggists, and butchers. This was indeed something new, for Naṣir-i-Khūsrau had written several years before that "the area between Cairo and Fostat was covered by water, except the sultan's garden, which was on a hill." The Pond of the Elephant still existed east of the canal, which flowed into it when the Nile rose.

This entire area, then, had become one large settlement that even extended beyond the two cities. Ibn Riḍwan wrote: "The capital of Egypt is divided into four parts: Fostat, Cairo, the island of Roḍah, and Giza. Muqaṭṭam Mountain is to the east, between the capital and the city cemeteries. The most important part is Fostat, which borders on the Nile to the west. On the western banks of the Nile there are trees of all sizes. The streets and alleys of Fostat are narrow, and its buildings are tall."

The geography of the site must be taken into consideration in any description of Fostat and Cairo, which had just been founded when Ibn Ḥawqal wrote: "Fostat is a very beautiful city located where the Nile separates into two branches. One passes from Fostat to the first bank, where there are beautiful buildings and large houses; this section is called Jazira, 'the island' (formerly known as Roḍah). One crosses on a bridge made up of about thirty boats; then a second bridge, similar to the first, spans another branch and leads from this island toward important buildings and homes erected on a third bank, called Giza. Fostat is a large city whose area is about one-third the size of Baghdad; it extends for about one parasang in a heavily populated and extremely fertile area. This city has other outstanding and agreeable qualities. Its neighborhoods have vast clearings, enormous market-places, imposing commercial centers, extensive privately owned lands, and, in addition, a splendid outward appearance, a pleasant atmosphere, and blooming gardens and green parks, regardless of the season.

"In Fostat the Arabs are grouped by tribes in neighborhoods bearing tribal names. Today there are fewer of these sections, most of them having disappeared. The land is saline and is not composed of pure soil. The houses have five, six, and even seven storeys, and occasionally up to two hundred people live in one building. Most of these constructions are built of unfired brick. The ground floor is generally uninhabited.

"Outside the city, there were formerly buildings erected by Aḥmad ibn Ṭūlūn in an area of one square mile, in which his troops were quartered. This site has fallen in ruins.

"People from the Maghrib have just founded, outside Fostat, a city which they have named Cairo. It was planned by Jauhar, the Maghrib general, at the time he entered Egypt, and is to be used by his army and his followers and as a place to store his supplies. It now contains living quarters and markets, as well as a place for raising cattle, and sites for such services as bathhouses and hotels. There are even well-built palaces and other useful installations. Jauhar surrounded it by a high, solid wall, which encloses an area three times larger than the built up section. This is a type of corral for the protection of livestock in case of danger. Within there are the administrative offices for Egypt and a beautiful and elegant cathedral mosque served by priests and muezzins."

For Moqaddasi, at the end of the tenth century, Fostat was a large city, heavily populated, of great renown and considerable importance, with a finer reputation than Baghdad's, famous for its markets and its bathhouses, with a greater population than Nishapur's, more illustrious than Basra, and vaster than Damascus. He added that the food was excellent and that fruit and vegetables were abundant and inexpensive. The city stretched along the Nile. Ships brought to its banks all sorts of products from the north and the south, and pavilions providing entertainment had sprung up there.

Ibn Riḍwan, as a physician, was severely critical of the city's sanitation: "One of the practices of the people of Fostat is to throw into the streets and alleys everything that dies in their houses: cats, dogs, and other domestic animals of that kind. They rot there, and this putrescence spreads through the air. Another one of their habits is to throw into the Nile, whose water they drink, the remains and the corpses of their animals. Their latrines empty into the Nile and sometimes obstruct the flow of the water. They, thus, drink this putrid matter mixed with their water. Another of the inconveniences in Fostat is the great number of bathhouse steamrooms, which give off into the air an excessive amount of smoke. Because of the heat, there is a great deal of dust which is irritating to the throat and dirties clean clothes in a single day. Whoever goes into the city on business comes back with his face and beard covered with quantities of dust. In the evening, especially in the summer, a troubled, blackish vapor hangs over the city. The dust is particularly thick when there

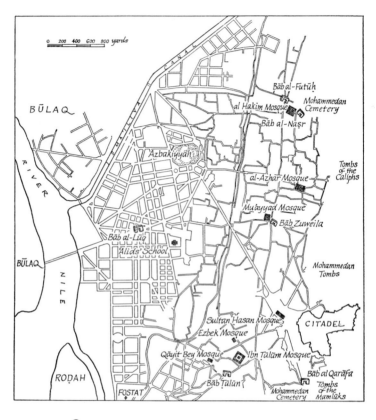

Map labels:
- BŪLAQ
- RIVER
- NILE
- BŪLAQ
- RODAH
- FOSTAT
- Azbakiyyah
- Bāb al-Lūq
- 'Alids' School
- Bāb al-Futūh
- al Hakim Mosque
- Mohammedan Cemetery
- Bāb al-Naṣr
- al-Azhar Mosque
- Tombs of the Caliphs
- Mu'ayyad Mosque
- Bāb Zuweila
- Mohammedan Tombs
- Sultan Hasan Mosque
- Ezbek Mosque
- CITADEL
- Qāyit Bey Mosque
- Ibn Tūlūn Mosque
- Bāb al Qarāfa
- Bāb Tūlūn
- Mohammedan Cemetery
- Tombs of the Mamlūks
- 0  200  400  600  800 yards

CAIRO, SHOWING ITS MAIN STREETS AND BUILDINGS
From Stanley Lane-Poole, *The Story of Cairo* (London, 1902)

is no wind in the air. The people of Fostat become used to this state of affairs, and this protects them from harm."

It may be wise to oppose this technical, troubled note with the enthusiastic view of a contemporary Persian traveler, whose testimony we have already examined: "When one views the city of Fostat from a distance, one has the impression of looking at a mountain. There are houses which are fourteen storeys high; others have only seven floors. A well-known merchant assured me that in Fostat there are a great number of houses where one can find rooms for rent. Certain market-places and streets are always lit up by lamps; since they are covered, they never receive the light of day.

"On the north side, there is a market called The Market of the Lamps. There is nothing similar to it in any other country. Rare and precious objects from all parts of the world are found here. I have seen shell products such as small boxes, combs, and knife handles. I have also noticed rock-crystal of great beauty, artistically designed by workmen who have a great deal of taste. I have seen elephant tusks from Zangebar. From Abyssinia, too, was brought a cowhide, resembling a leopard skin; slippers were made from this. From this same country came a large sized domestic bird; its feathers are spotted with white and on its head it has a crest like a peacock's.

"All types of porcelain are made in Fostat. It is so fine and transparent that a hand held outside a vase can be seen through it. Bowls, cups, dishes, and other utensils are made here. They are decorated with colors whose shades change with the position of the object. A transparent and very pure glass which resembles the emerald is manufactured here; it is sold by weight.

"The city of Fostat stretches along the banks of the Nile.

On the riverbank there are a great number of kiosks and pavilions that provide entertainment. Here, with the aid of a rope, one can draw water from the Nile, which furnishes the total supply for the city. Water-carriers transport it in goatskin bottles, either on camel back or on their own shoulders. Staples are unloaded from the boats at the very doorsteps of the grocers. Because of the crowds in the streets, it would be impossible to have beasts of burden transport these products.

"Opposite Fostat, in the middle of the river, toward the west, there is an island on which a city had formerly been built. It is a rock rising out of the middle of the Nile, which separates into two branches, each of which, in my estimation, is as wide as the Oxus; but the current is smoother and slower. Fostat is connected to this island by a bridge made of thirty-six boats. One part of the city is situated on the other side of the river; it is called Giza; there is no bridge to it, and the Nile is crossed by boat or ferry.

"The merchants sell at a fixed price. In the bazar, druggists, grocers, and hardware dealers furnish the glasses, porcelain containers, and paper to hold or wrap what they sell.

"The dealers and merchants ride saddled donkeys between their homes and the bazar. At the entrance of each street and each market are found donkeys with pretty saddles. They can be ridden at any time at little cost. It is said that there are fifty thousand of them that can be rented by the public every day. Military men and valets attached to the army are the only ones who ride horses. Merchants, peasants, artisans, and government employees ride donkeys.

"I have seen so much wealth in Fostat that if I tried to list it or describe it, my words would not be believed. I have found it impossible to count it or estimate it."

Finally, the work of the geographer Idrīsi, in the middle of the following century, shows that the founding of Cairo did not hurt the prosperity of Fostat; rather the contrary was true: "It is a very important city, whether considered from the point of view of its size and population or the abundance of the comforts of life and everything that is beautiful and good. The streets are wide, the buildings solid, the markets well supplied and busy, and the cultivated fields adjoin each other and are renowned for their fertility. As for the inhabitants, they are outstanding for the high level of their thoughts and aspirations, as well as for their piety; they possess great wealth, which is always increasing, and the most beautiful merchandise; they are neither bothered by cares nor devoured by worry, for they enjoy great security and perfect tranquility, since public authority protects them and justice reigns among them. Fostat is generally well populated, and its bazars are well furnished with all sorts of food, drink and beautiful clothing. The inhabitants enjoy affluence and are distinguished by their elegance and the gentleness of their manners."

The city was for a time condemned by the Fatimid vizier Shāwar, in 1168, when it was besieged by the Frankish armies, for he wanted to concentrate all his forces for the defense of Cairo. He, therefore, ordered that no one was to remain in Old Cairo. An Arab wrote: "The people left in great haste, abandoning their possessions and their goods, in order to save themselves and their children. There was an impetuous flow of human beings; it seemed as though they were leaving their tombs for the Last Judgment. Fathers neglected their children, and brothers were not each other's keepers. They went so far as to pay twenty dinars for a mount to take them from Fostat to Cairo. They camped in the mosques of Cairo, in the bathhouses, in the streets, and on roads. There they were, thrown together pell-mell with their wives and children, having lost their possessions and waiting for the enemy to bear down on Cairo. Shāwar had twenty thousand pots of naphtha and ten thousand fire-brands brought into Fostat. All of these were spread out in the city, and the flames and the smoke of the fire rose to the heavens. It was a frightening spectacle. The fire continued in the houses of Old Cairo for fifty-four entire days, as did the organized pillage carried out by slaves and sailors. For a long time after that, Fostat was a ruin called 'the hills of debris.' "

# 3
## Saladin

HAVING PUT AN END to the reign of the Fatimids, Saladin tried to find a fortified place for his residence. It is said that he chose the site where the Citadel is now located because he had noticed that meat spoiled within twenty-four hours when hung in the Citadel area. He, therefore, ordered a citadel to be built on the Muqaṭṭam spur, which juts out like a peninsula. The mosques and tombs located there were destroyed, and the little pyramids of Giza, which we are assured were very numerous, were demolished. The remaining stones were moved and were used to build the Citadel of Cairo. The sultan's intention was for a single wall to enclose Cairo, Fostat, and the Citadel, but he died before the wall and the Citadel were finished. Begun in 1176, work on the Citadel was completed in 1207; the wall was never finished. Maqrīzi comes to the following conclusion: "Living in what he considered a conquered country, fearing uprisings provoked by the partisans of the Fatimids, who were supported by the Christians, Saladin very prudently desired the same thing as the founders of al-ʿAskar, Katai, and Cairo. He wanted to abandon the residences of his predecessors and establish the new dynasty in a setting worthy of it, far from the populous sections. It was a question of security. This is the habit of kings; they always efface the traces of those who came before them. This is why they have destroyed most of the cities and fortresses. This is how they behaved before Islam and during the time of Islam."

Saladin, therefore, changed the character of the Fatimid city, which had been a fortress, and made it a place where the common people and the general population could build homes. He reduced the size of the caliph's palace, a part of which was demolished and another part converted into private homes.

The Citadel remains the symbol of the great Saladin's reign, even though the sovereign never lived in it. It stands as a tangible memorial to an outstanding figure, a man ahead of his time and superior to both his coreligionists and his enemies, who considered him a being of moderate and loyal temperament, inspired by pure and unselfish motives—in short, a remarkable person.

When the Citadel was founded in Cairo, it stood as a useless challenge to a peaceful population, which never rebelled in the capital and stirred in the provinces only at times when the tax authorities were a little too indiscreet.

In any event, the founding of the Citadel was a break with the past, a very sharp one since it represented a probable change of customs and an upsetting of the social structure. By its obvious location, if nothing else, the Citadel constituted a theatrical and spectacular shock. The centers of government remained shut up behind walls, protected against possible revolts. At first there was the fear of an unsubmissive population; then, after the creation of mercenary armies, the desire to keep them from too much contact with the natives; finally we shall see, under the Mamlūk sultans, the wish to protect the ruling faction against the constantly seething dissidents. Once the Citadel was erected, the city of Cairo began to give itself more breathing space by demolishing part of the Fatimid ramparts or, as was the case in the northern area, by building new houses up against them.

Ibn Ṭūlūn's city had been a princely residence; this same term can even be applied to Fatimid Cairo. It is truly with the arrival of Saladin that an Egyptian metropolis, a capital, was created. The glory of Cairo, without underestimating the Fatimids, dates from the time of the Ayyūbids. The Spanish traveler Ibn Jubayr knew when a so-called city was not really one at all. In speaking of a town in Upper Mesopotamia, he declared: "This town shows as much taste for Bedouin habits as it does indifference for city manners: no wall to defend it, no well-built houses to adorn it. It stands in the midst of the surrounding countryside like a talisman guarding its crops."

It was, therefore, with a certain degree of pride that he described the building site of the Citadel at the height of activity in 1183: "We visited the buildings of the Citadel, a fortress with strong defensive works, which is within the limits of Cairo, and where the sultan intends to make his residence. He is having the wall lengthened in order to unite the two cities of Miṣr and Cairo. The construction workers and the people in charge of carrying out the work and furnishing the vast amount of material, including the sawing of marble, the cutting of large stones, the digging into rock with picks to build the moat surrounding the fortress wall, a job which is one of those wonders which will leave a lasting impression, these workers are Christian prisoners whose number is incalculable. They are the only ones who may be employed in this work."

The middle-class homes of the city amazed the physician 'Abd al-Laṭīf. He gives us some interesting information about them which could explain why the rooms found on the same floor are never on the same level: "When someone wants to build a house, a palace for a prince, or a market, he calls an engineer and assigns him the job. The engineer goes to the site, which is either on raised land or some other place, divides it mentally, and makes all his plans, depending on the nature of the building that has been ordered. After this, he begins and completely finishes each section, before starting another, so that each part can be used and lived in as soon as it is ready, before the entire building is done. When one part is finished, he starts another, and so on, until the entire project is finished by the joining of all the parts without any error in the over-all work, and without any empty space or omissions which would have to be rectified afterward."

He adds: "A marvelous art and a very wise arrangement of all the sections are noticed in the Egyptians' buildings. They rarely leave any space that is useless or does not have its purpose. Their palaces are vast. They generally live on the upper floors. The windows of their homes face the north and are exposed to the most agreeable winds. There is hardly a house without a ventilator; these ventilators are large, wide, and take advantage of any wind. They are arranged with a great deal of art."

From the Ayyūbid period on, the city of Cairo follows precise laws concerning its development, which result from its growth in population. Toward the south, Cairo tends to join Fostat, needed by the new capital as a port on the Nile. But between the two cities beautiful gardens will last until the beginning of the fourteenth century. On the west, the city grows toward the banks of the Nile and crosses the canal, so that the island of Būlaq becomes the new river front and rivals Fostat as a commercial port. Thus, the development of Cairo will not hurt the old city of Fostat or cause its decadence; it will simply change its role.

Ibn Jubayr wrote: "The city of Fostat is still marked by

the ruin caused by the fire during the troubled period at the time of the fall of the Fatimid dynasty in the year 1169. But most of it is rebuilt today, and there are whole lines of un-interrupted buildings. It is a big city."

We have just referred to the account of a Spanish pilgrim, and we are going to continue with a description given by a traveler of the same nationality, Ibn Sa'īd. His is a lively account, full of witty asides. He notices, first of all, the filth of the old city: "It rarely rains; the feet of the passers-by stir up the dust, which is of an ugly color, and which dirties the walls. Because of that, the air is bad. The markets are con-gested, because they are narrow. They are built of reeds and fired bricks and are several storeys high."

He adds: "When I lived in Cairo, I had a keen desire to see Fostat with my own eyes. I was accompanied by a de-termined man. At Bāb Zuweila, I saw more donkeys than can be found in any other country, as far as I know; they were for the use of anyone going to Fostat. My companion climbed on a donkey and motioned me to do the same. But I refused because of the habits which I had acquired in the Maghrib. He informed me that Egyptian notables did not find this degrading, and, indeed, I noticed jurists, cloth merchants, and distinguished persons riding donkeys. I followed their example, but while I was getting myself properly seated, the renter of these animals gave a signal to his donkey, who began to run rapidly and kick up a blackish dust that blinded me and soiled my clothes. What I had feared then happened. Because of my lack of practice in the art of riding a donkey, because of the sudden and unexpected violent departure of my animal, and also because of the donkey-driver's disagree-able attitude, I fell into the black swirl of dust.

"I paid the driver what I owed him and said, 'It would be

very kind of you if you let me continue on foot.' I finally found the road again and walked about two miles. When I got to Fostat, all joy abandoned me. I gazed upon black, dilapidated walls and a dusty horizon. I entered by a broken-down gate which could not be locked and walked into the rubbish thrown among buildings placed askew in narrow, winding streets. These buildings were made of black brick, reeds, and palm trunks and had one storey piled up on another. Around the doors there were black humus and garbage which suffocate a fastidious person and offend the eye of an elegant man. Going on my way, I came to some narrow markets. It is impossible to estimate the dense crowd of people, the piles of merchandise, and the goatskin bottles brought in on camels. Finally, I arrived at the cathedral mosque closed in by markets, a startling contrast with what I had been able to see in Seville and Marrakech. I entered and saw a mosque of beautiful dimensions and ancient construction, which had no paneling; poorly cared for mats hung from the walls and lay on the floor. The crowd which crossed the building from one door to the other had left a path which served as a shortcut. Here merchants sold all sorts of sweets, cakes, and other dainties that the customers ate on the spot without any shame, for this had become their habit. A great number of little boys carried jars of water which they passed around among the people who were eating and who threw their refuse on the ground in the corners. The spiders had woven many webs on the ceilings, in the corners, and on the walls. Children played in the court. The walls were marked with the vulgar lines of various graffiti, done in coal and brick and traced by people of the lowest class. Yet, in spite of everything, in this building one breathed an air of joy, of happiness with life, of peace of soul that was not encountered in the great mosque of Seville, with its rich paneling and its garden in the central court. I thought about this strange charm that came through, the reasons for which was not immediately understood; I learned that it was due to a mysterious grace conferred by the Companions of the Prophet, who were present when the temple was founded. I saw in many places circles of classes where reading of the Koran, jurisprudence, and grammar were taught. I asked people who were informed about the source of income and was told that it was mainly through tithing and the collectors were disturbed, because they had to resort to force and threats.

"We left there to go to the banks of the Nile. I saw a dirty riverside of blackish earth, where space was limited and developed in a meandering fashion, and there was not a single white wall; buildings were set up for the construction of boats and the storing of merchandise. A bridge, which is not very long, connects this bank with the isle of Roḍah, and on the other side another bridge leads from the island to Giza. But, since the sultan has built a citadel on Roḍah, the people are not permitted to use these bridges; they cross the river in boats. In any event, they are forbidden to go over on horseback.

"In no country have I seen people who are friendlier than the inhabitants of Fostat; they are much more pleasant than the people of Cairo, which is only about two miles away. It would take too long to dwell upon the qualities of courtesy, graciousness, and kindness in their relations, shown by the inhabitants of Fostat.

"It would be impossible to estimate the quantity of merchandise unloaded in Fostat coming from the Alexandrian and the Hejaz seas. Various factories such as sugar refineries and soap-works have been built in Fostat, for Cairo was especially constructed for the army. Thus the military establishment is more important in Cairo than in Fostat; also workshops devoted to weaving, dying, and luxury items destined for the state are more sumptuous in Cairo."

In another passage, Ibn Sa'īd gives mild praise to Cairo: "The city of Cairo is a brilliant, splendid town, which the Fatimids outdid each other to embellish and which they created and chose for the residence of their caliphs and the center of their hope. Fostat was forgotten by them and was abandoned, after it had known a period of enthusiasm. Cairo's fame is greater than the city itself; its arrangement and its buildings must have been different from what I saw. The caliphs had devoted all their effort to their palaces; it was from here that they reigned. They also had, on the Canal, immense structures whose remains are still magnificent.

"The place in Cairo called Bain al-Qaṣreyn, 'Between the Two Palaces,' is laid out in a manner worthy of sovereigns; there is a spacious square for the army and for strollers. If everything were like that, Cairo would be notable for its squares, and its conception would be worthy of a monarch. But this is just a little zone; from there one comes upon narrow streets and dusty passages, squeezed between shops, streets where horses and pedestrians are crowded together. It is enough to leave you gasping for breath. One day I saw a minister go by, accompanied by important officials, and followed by a great retinue. Into his path came an ox wagon, loaded with stones, which blocked all the exits of the shops. The vizier stopped; the scurrying became intense. This happened in a place where there were cook-shops, and the smoke blew onto the face and the clothing of the minister. The passers-by, I among them, almost died. Most of the streets of Cairo, you can see, are narrow, dark, and full of dust and sweepings. The buildings which tower above them are made of reeds and earth, are very high, and have between them only a narrow passageway for air and light. In no city of the Maghrib have I seen alleys worse than these. As I walked, my chest became constricted and I was terribly distressed until I came to Bain al-Qaṣreyn.

"In addition, this city which is on the Nile, is still so far from it that the population is dying of thirst; yet, it was feared that the river would invade the city and destroy the houses. When one wants to enjoy a view of the river, one has to go a long way into the suburbs, in the sections built up in the outlying areas, where the air is always troubled by the black dust stirred up by the feet of the pedestrians.

"When the traveler arrives in this manner at the place called Maqs, he sees a dirty, black wall; in the midst of this dusty atmosphere, his soul shrinks and he becomes a misanthrope.

"In this suburb, I found the Pond of the Elephant pleasing because it is as round as the full moon, and the pavilions which are above it are like stars. The sultan often sails here. The owners light up their pavilions according to their fantasy or their means. That gives it a pleasant appearance.

"Fostat is rich in staples which are sold at a lower price than in Cairo because of the proximity of the Nile. It is there that the ships transporting merchandise stop, and everything that comes in is sold in the neighborhood. This does not happen on the Cairo river front, which is too far from the city. But Cairo is more prosperous and more luxurious than Fostat, because it has more beautiful schools, more crowded *khans*, and more important homes of emirs. The sultanate is, indeed, more partial to it because of its closeness to the

Citadel; all government services are easier and more numerous here.

"In our time, however, since the sultan has decided to build the fortress of Roḍah, across from Fostat, and to make it the center of the sultanate, the prosperity of Fostat has grown; a great number of officers have moved there, and the markets have become crowded. The sultan has built, opposite the bridge leading to the island, a spacious market, and he has transferred from Cairo the market reserved for the troops, where furs, cloth, and other such things are sold.

"There are cooks in Cairo who acquired their skill from the practices of the palaces of the Fatimid caliphs; they perform their work with admirable art and first-rate ability. Very beautiful leather objects, which are exported to Syria, are made in Cairo. There are many skillful bow makers. All sorts of belts, leather bags, straps, and other products of that type are sent from Cairo to Syria. In addition, Cairo today is big and well populated and has such an abundance of things that only the Creator of the universe can count them.

"It is a city within the means of the poor man thanks to the abundance and the low price of bread, the existence of concerts and entertainment within and outside the city, and the easy fulfilment of his desires. He does as he pleases, dancing in the markets, going about naked, and getting drunk on hashish and other products. None of the poor is forced to serve in the navy, except those who are from the Maghrib; this service is required of them because of their knowledge of navigation.

"I went into the Canal neighborhood. I saw many strange things there. Drunkenness is the cause of murders; therefore, drinking is prohibited during certain periods. The Canal is confined on both sides by pavilions which are crowded with people who devote their time to having fun, carousing, and reveling so that people of respectable habits and important people do not venture to cross it by boat. At night, the lamps on both banks offer a charming spectacle. Many well-bred people walk here at night."

\* \* \*

Saladin's Sunnite reaction resulted in the creation of a new religious institution, the madrasah. Nothing can make us feel the scope of this reform better than the text of one of the earliest Ayyūbid inscriptions in Cairo:

"This madrasah was built at the behest of the sheik, of the doctor, of the imam, of the ascetic Nadjm al-Dīn, the pillar of Islam, the model of human beings, the mufti of the sects, Abul-Barakāt, the son of Muwaffaq, and Khabushani to be used by the jurists who are disciples of Shāfi'ī and are characterized by their firm basic doctrine, and to be united by al-Ash'ari's method in opposition to vain reasoners and innovators. The building was finished in the month of Ramadān of the year 575 (February 1180)."

Severe qualifications are attached to the religious theses of the fallen regime, for in Islam all innovation is erroneous. The inscription points up the importance of the founder of one of the four orthodox rites, the imam Shāfi'ī whose influence is still felt in Egypt. Saladin did not spare any efforts in his work on Shāfi'ī's mausoleum; one can still admire today the splendid wooden cenotaph that he built. For Ibn Jubayr, Shāfi'ī's sepulcher was "one of the most important and one of the vastest memorials; near it was built a school which no other founded in this country equals in size, dimensions, or importance. When one walks around it, one imagines that it is an independent city."

Al-Ash'ari, the last person named in the inscription, was the great Mesopotamian scholar who founded Islam's dogmatic theology. The madrasah was one of the instruments of the movement which he began. Al-Ash'ari used Aristotelian logic in setting the dogmas of Islam, but we must be careful to notice that his position, like that of Moslem orthodoxy which came after him, can be summarized in these words: "God appeals to human reason in order to be understood, but he is not to be judged by it." Al-Ash'ari was claimed by the devout group, and his actions precipitated the decadence of Moslem intellectual life. His pietistic severity could only shackle thought, and his ideas were imposed like a catechism which was not to tolerate any discussion.

The institution of the madrasah, the religious school, was perhaps of vital necessity to the future of Islam, whose doctrine was menaced by schisms and heresy and whose possessions were threatened by the Crusaders. The result, nevertheless, was the very rapid loss of quality in education. The madrasah was introduced into Egypt by Saladin, and because of its controlled instruction religious and philosophic dissension came to an end, as did the cult of antiquity extolled by the Fatimids. New programs, inspired only by Sunnite thought, were to establish orthodoxy definitely. This, moreover, was far removed from the pious men of early Islam who taught through divine love and professional honor. From now on we find officials who hand out standard lessons to students who are eager for diplomas so that they, too, can serve the state.

The beginnings were stirring, according to Ibn Jubayr, who was enthusiastic over the institutions created by Saladin: "The schools and monasteries were founded for studious and religious people who come here from the most distant countries. Each one of them finds a place to live, an instructor to teach him the field of learning which he desires to master, and a sum of money to take care of all his needs. The sultan has extended his solicitude for these strangers, who have come such a great distance, to the point of building bathhouses where they can bathe and a hospital where their sick can be cared for. There are physicians assigned to check on their state of health, and under their orders, there are assistants who see to it that the treatments and diets prescribed for their welfare are carried out. There are also people appointed to visit the sick, especially among foreigners, who do not choose to go to the hospital; these people explain the cases so the doctors can take over the treatment.

"It was also through very noble motives that the sultan was led to give two loaves of bread a day to the strangers, regardless of their number, found wandering along the roadsides. He has designated a man in whom he has confidence, and who acts in his name, to supervise this daily distribution. The number of loaves of bread amounts to two thousand or more each day, depending upon how great or small the number of supplicants is."

Thus, we read the picturesque descriptions of Egypt written by the Spaniards Ibn Jubayr and Ibn Sa'īd; we should associate with them a Mesopotamian physician, 'Abd al-Laṭīf, a great scholar, who lived for rather a long time in Syria and in Egypt, where he came in contact with Maimonides. We have his account of Egypt in which he gives evidence of his profound knowledge of natural history. In Cairo he had the opportunity to examine the skeletons of mummies, and he quite proudly tells us of his direct observations. He acquires on "the shape of the bones, their joints, their sockets, their respective proportions and their positions knowledge that books would never have offered, for there is a great difference between a description and firsthand observation of things."

We should not attach too much importance to the relationship of Emperor Frederick II with the scholars of the East. But if it did not advance the cause of knowledge, it did give evidence of a desire for contact and of homage paid to the Orient by the West. We know that Frederick, fascinated by philosophy, mathematics, and astronomy, had asked the sultan al-Malik al-Kāmil to have answered certain questions which preoccupied the emperor. The names of several scholars—curiously, some of them are professional jurists—are obtained in this way, but only their vast knowledge, and nothing else, is spoken of. Perhaps an exception should be made of Qarafi, who solved some problems in optics.

One last physician, Ibn al-Nafīs, who has become known because of recent studies of unsuccessful work on pulmonary circulation, ended his career in Cairo. But the physicians of the East no longer had the qualifications to take advantage of his presence.

Finally, Cairo is honored by the presence of the poet Ibn al-Fāriḍ, who became drunk on wine and loved to sing of annihilation in God. The pantheism of Ibn al-Fāriḍ has been spoken of; this is probably "a manner of feeling, not a system of thought." He was the first lyric poet of mysticism, creating a form which was to remain classic. His originality consisted of writing ambiguous verse which, instead of being seen as erotic symbolism, was interpreted as applying to profane love; this perhaps increased his popularity. In any event, his poetry places us in the presence of the most beautiful mystic hymns. His language is difficult, if only because of the abundance of allegories and Ibn al-Fāriḍ's inability to resist a certain tendency toward preciosity and the abuse of poetic procedure.

# 4

## The Mamlūk Sultans:
## General View and Social Aspects

WE CAN WELL IMAGINE the astonishment of the medieval European traveler standing on top of the Muqaṭṭam. We are told that here was one of the most beautiful views in the world. The splendor of the panorama was increased by the incalculable number of cupolas and minarets, which added agreeable variety to the uniformity of the city whose roofs were all flat. The background was formed by the pyramids, which, like mountain peaks, were lost in a milky haze.

One of these travelers wrote: "I remember one of many times that I sat for more than a quarter of an hour on the rock outside the castle gate. Discovering Cairo from a height is one of the most agreeable sights. This pleasure comes from the multitude of white mosque towers, each of which has three or four rows of balusters. These towers seem to be interlaced with the beautiful green of the numerous palm trees growing in various city gardens; all of this joined together makes for a certain harmony and charming diversity which is greatly pleasing to the eye. The grandeur of the river, which during the flood season forms a lake larger than the eye can see, the multitude of islands which animate and diversify this silvery plain, and the haughty majesty of the mountains bordering this cheerful site, all give this scene unequaled nobility and variety."

There was good reason to be impressed by this colossal metropolis which strecthed out into the shape of a half-moon from the imam Shāfiʿī's mausoleum to the tombs of the caliphs. In the Middle Ages, the city was composed of four very different urban centers: Cairo, the Fatimid city itself, partly surrounded by walls which were disappearing day by day behind parasite constructions; Old Cairo on the site of ancient Fostat; Būlaq, a former island which had recently become part of Cairo and was the commercial port on the Nile; and finally, the cemeteries of Qarāfa, to the north and south of the Citadel. Certain suburbs, such as those of Bāb al-Lūq, Zuweila, and the Ibn Ṭūlūn mosque, should not be overlooked.

Cairo and Old Cairo were indeed one, since there was no separation between the two, except for a small area of uncultivated, uninhabited land which was more or less deserted in spots. In some places the distance between the houses of Cairo and those of Old Cairo were within crossbow range of each other; in other places they were separated by twice that distance. Some areas between the two more or less important agglomerations consisted of vast and sumptuous orchards, vegetable plots, and pleasure gardens. Going from Matariya to Cairo in 1483, Breydenbach found on his right some very beautiful gardens planted with fruit-bearing trees in the midst of which rose fortress-like palaces. The gardens and the houses extended in an uninterrupted line to Cairo. Pierre Belon entered the city through Būlaq and noticed a great number of trees for the distance of one-half league.

Cairo had begun to grow larger from the end of the Fatimid regime. Doubtless at the beginning new homes arose because the city was overpopulated and was swelling and bursting beyond the walls; the still existing gates, especially Bāb Zuweila, had for quite some time found themselves inside the city, exactly as happened in Paris where the arches of triumph mark the sites of the St. Denis and St. Martin gates. The Arab texts of the fifteenth century speak of the Bāb Zuweila suburb as being an integral part of Cairo; this again is the same as in Paris with its *faubourgs* Poissonnière and St. Denis.

Later there was a different phenomenon as the city joined the Citadel; eventually the Citadel was no longer isolated as many buildings, especially at the end of the fourteenth century, connected it with the city.

Marcel Clerget very correctly wrote: "The creation of the citadel had a very strong repercussion on the nearby neighborhoods. Encroaching on the cemeteries, the suburbs soon spread to the foot of the citadel. One of the most important market-places of any Arab town, the one where horses, donkeys, and camels are sold, was transferred to Rumeyla. On the site of the area formerly occupied by the Fatimid army units were installed vast gardens and pools; this suburb assumed a much more agreeable appearance and was enjoyed by the inhabitants of the Citadel. In the west, other gardens then appeared, especially at Bāb al-Lūq, making of these neighborhoods a sort of park which was to last, in part, under the reign of the Mamlūks."

This expansion was to continue to the south as well as to the north, beyond the Bāb al-Naṣr and the Bāb al-Futūḥ gates, and there was a considerable amount of construction in the new Ḥusainiyya section. In the same way, many houses were built along the Pond of the Elephant and both banks of the canal. Crossing this canal were bridges of one or two broken arches, narrow roadbeds, and high ramparts. When the canal was full, its banks, lined with buildings with their latticework windows, must have been very picturesque.

*       *       *

As a whole this group of different cities, which together formed what medieval European travelers called Great Cairo, did quite well economically, situated as it was on commercial crossroads. The east-west road was used for commerce between Africa and Asia and for African Moslems' pilgrimages to Mecca. The other route brought to Cairo a great quantity of costly merchandise which arrived overland in Egypt from central Africa and Abyssinia; and by sea there also came to Cairo from India and China a flood of rare products, which made their way on the Nile to Alexandria, where Europeans came to buy them.

Thus, Cairo became a magnificent commercial center, a type of wonderful turntable, from which imports from the Far East were sent out along the sea lanes of the Mediterranean. This was the golden age of the spice merchants. Piloti's remarks point this out: "Whoever is the lord of Cairo can call himself the lord and master of Christendom, and he is also the lord of all the islands and countries where spices are produced; this is the reason why no spice products can go to or be sold in any country but the sultan's. For Cairo stands between two seas; it has first of all the Western Sea, on whose shores are Alexandria, Damietta, Jaffa, Beirut, and all of Syria. It then has the sea which is on the other side of the country, as is Jedda, the port of Mecca. From there, merchandise travels from place to place along the coast and then comes to Tor, where one finds the port of Mount Sinai; camels which leave Mecca come to this coast and unload at this port. This coast, from Mecca to the port of Mount Sinai, is under the authority of the sultan of Cairo. Thus, the sultan's country is between two seas like an island and controls India and the West. There is no other way for the ships coming from the Indies to sail, and their merchants can sell in no country but the sultan of Cairo's. The same is true for the Christians of the West. And you, therefore, know that it is always essential to be on excellent terms with the sultan if we want to sell or buy in his country, or if we want to go to Jerusalem on a pilgrimage."

Navigation on the Nile in the Middle Ages was strikingly important and rapid. A passage of rather sustained lyricism attests to this: "Do not forget the ships with their sails standing high like banners which, when the wind is favorable, go faster than the best arrows. They are decorated with red gold, or painted in many brilliant colors like spotted serpents, versicolored fruits, peacocks, or like ancient hypogea. Carried on the current of the surging waters, they remind us of Noah's remarkable ark as they move forward. When the wings of their sails open, they fly ahead of the speeding wind or the rapidly developing cloud. Thrusting upward with the vultures toward the clouds, they swim in the waves with the fish."

It was essentially through navigation on the Nile, which was always very active, that the capital received its supplies. Ibn Sa'īd saw on the Nile an amazing number of ships bringing from the Alexandrian Sea and the Sea of Hejaz merchandise which came from all parts of the world. One hundred years later, Ibn Baṭṭuṭah was still very enthusiastic: "One sees upon the Nile thirty-six thousand ships belonging to the sultan and his subjects. These ships go back and forth, upriver toward Upper Egypt and downriver toward Alexandria and Damietta, with merchandise and staples which are sold at advantageous prices. No one sailing on the Nile has to carry provisions with him, since any time he wants to land on the riverbank he can do so, either to attend to his ablutions, to pray, or to buy food and other products."

A little later Frescobaldi was to say: "The Nile flows along one side of the city, and there is a good port. When we were there, there was such a great quantity of boats that all those that I have ever seen in the ports of Genoa, Venice, and Ancona put together, not counting the double-decked ships, would not come to one-third the number of those which were there, all of which amounted to four hundred boats or more."

If we are to believe Pierre Belon: "The *germes*, boats, and other types of vessels land at the village of Bulak to unload what they bring to Cairo. We observed ships of the Nile, called *germes*, which are of three or four different types. Some of them are low, flat, and wide, but almost round in shape. The largest would be quite similar to the boats on the Seine, except that they are much shorter. They carry much greater loads than the others. They have lateen sails. The smallest ones, which have square sails, do not go very far from Bulak; they are used merely to cross the Nile, to carry provisions from Cairo to the villages, and to transport livestock from one bank to the other. The *germes* which go as far as Damietta and Alexandria have lateen sails and can enter a calm sea in clement weather."

\* \* \*

Ibn Khaldūn wrote: "He who has not seen Cairo does not know the grandeur of Islam. It is the metropolis of the universe, the garden of the world, the ant-hill of the human species, the portico of Islam, the throne of royalty, a city embellished with castles and palaces, decorated with dervish monasteries and with schools, and lighted by the moons and stars of erudition. A paradise extends on each bank of the Nile; the flow of its waters replaces, for the inhabitants, the water from the sky, while the fruit and the wealth of the earth offer them their salutations. I went through the crowded streets of this capital and through its markets, which burst with all the delights of this life. One could talk forever of a city which gives evidence of so many resources and furnishes so much proof of the most advanced civilization. Formerly, I had asked my teachers and my fellow-students, after their return from a pilgrimage, what they thought of Cairo; I had also questioned merchants, and their answers, although of different forms, were basically the same. One of them told me, 'What one sees in a dream surpasses reality, but all that one could dream about Cairo would not come up to the truth.'"

This bit of lyricism is perfectly suitable as a preamble to the description of the Egyptian capital under the Mamlūk sultans. We should remark that not all the information given in the passage is exact, even if the historian thinks he is obliged to add: "Among the cities with the highest degree of civilization, Cairo would stand out as a source of science and art." But in the fourteenth and fifteenth centuries, Cairo, which had never been a center of learning comparable to Baghdad or Cordova, was an administrative and political center and, especially, a commercial focal point, which, while maintaining its artistic taste on a high level, was second-rate in things intellectual. Doubtless, Cairo's schools continued to furnish conscientious teachers, and that is probably what Ibn Khaldūn means when he states that "the good traditions in education have been maintained." There were unquestionably local celebrities, men of letters who were discussed, and, of course, the schools and monasteries did not lack teachers of holy scripture and of Koran reading, or even of history. They gave lessons to pupils whose ambition it was to succeed their teachers.

Under the regime of the Mamlūk sultans, the proliferation

of religious schools and monasteries should not deceive us. It has no relationship with the quality of the teachers; not a single great name has remained. These many educational establishments produced no man of real ability, no writer of talent; they were nothing but training schools for teachers. Aside from the *Prolegomena* by Ibn Khaldūn, that extraordinary scholar who was not trained in Egypt, no original work was produced in Cairo. This was the century of encyclopedists, authors of biographies which were often without interest, and compilers; there were never any original works. These were people who deserved in their time laudatory epitaphs and biographical sketches full of sonorous adjectives, but whose names quickly fell into complete oblivion. This makes us think of Balzac's reflection: "The glory of surgeons resembles that of actors, who exist only during their lifetime and whose talent is no longer appreciated after they have disappeared." In the fifteenth century Maqrīzi speaks of a "young teacher who resembled a human being only by his shape and who could be distinguished from an animal only by his ability to speak. Little by little, the courses in the school where he taught stopped completely." This drying up of the creative genius of Arab writers was not sudden. Already in the eleventh century a certain author is proud of having "had the merit, in putting his book together, of making a wise choice; the art of choosing is part of man's intelligence." Two centuries later this notion had become universal. Another writer says: "Composing today is nothing but gathering up what is dispersed and putting together what has fallen apart." These are only remarks and not the beginning of a case against Cairo, for I believe with William Marçais that "literature is not all of civilization." Monuments and objects of art are enough to perpetuate the glory of the Mamlūk sultans.

65

Thus, in this great movement of men in Egypt, and especially in Cairo, merchandise plays a more important role than ideas. There is the creation of merchant *bourgeoisie* eager for good food and a certain amount of comfort. It is in this sense that the people of Cairo can attain a higher standard of living. Their capital has become a market of international importance, and their world-wide trade has had considerable influence on the growth of the city.

\* \* \*

The historian Maqrīzi divides the Egyptian population into seven categories; although this division is rather artificial, it is somewhat interesting. The categories include: the officers of the kingdom and the high officials; the wealthy merchants, persons favored by fortune; the well-off tradesmen, such as the cloth merchants, the food dealers, the shopkeepers in the markets, or what can be called the lower middle class; the farmers, specialists in cultivation and plowing—in other words, the villagers and the country people; members of the religious orders, teachers and students—probably judges, too—notaries public, and soldiers of the guard; artisans, skilled workers, employees, porters, grooms, weavers, masons, and various types of laborers; the indigent, beggars, and the wretchedly poor. From all evidence, these were not closed castes from which there was no escape. The one exception was the Mamlūks, who constituted a privileged class above the very mixed population, whose members had nothing in common to defend. There was so little social hierarchy that in the same family there were merchants, artisans, and teachers; we know that business and teaching of religion were sometimes interchangeable and never incompatible professions. The people were not, therefore, obliged to remain in their social class. Financial failures played their part in this social mobility; there were some arrests and confiscation of fortunes. Rises in fortune were less frequent, but they occurred. Take, for example, the descendant of a Delta peasant, who sat astride his donkey as he sold unbleached cloth and materials in the market places; he was a mere peddler. After his death, his estate amounted to twenty thousand dinars in cash, without counting a large number of livestock.

Because of their humble origin, their training, and their education, the Mamlūks maintained a militaristic spirit which knew no pity; although they were unprejudiced, their warlike nature could not help but be prejudicial to public peace. The history of the Mamlūk officers lays bare their ambition, used to further perilous careers and dominated by anxiety for the future. Their actions, which reveal their arrogance and their debauchery, can be explained only as motivated by selfishness. Maqrīzi wrote: "The Mamlūks were responsible for much disorder in Egypt. They attacked the inhabitants, slaughtered them, pillaged their wealth, and carried off their wives. They engaged in such excess that even Europeans, had they been masters of the country, could not have done as much." Like professional soldiers of all periods and all countries, the Mamlūks were adventurers; we mean that they not only had a penchant for adventure and risk but were inclined to go too far in their intemperance. It is too bad that their partisan quarrels most often resulted only in wasted energy.

Men, sold into Egypt like the most common goods and freed by masters who were former slaves themselves, developed a new personality, under an assumed name, and tried to contribute to the grandeur of Moslem civilization. The Mamlūks gave the country a complicated, but efficient, administration. They had an army whose elements disrupted domestic politics, like the Grandes Compagnies during the Hundred Years' War, but which was of proven bravery and was often successful in battle. Egypt was governed by an oligarchy of lost children, who were worried about their privileges and imbued with their own prestige, as can be seen from their fabulous uniforms. It was a very closed society in which the right to power did not devolve from the prerogatives of birth, culture, or fortune, since no one who had not begun in servitude could become a sultan. In this strange society the freed slave could reach the highest honors of the state, but the free man in the country was bound to the soil in serfdom. This definition by Chateaubriand can be applied better to the Mamlūk regime than to ancient France: "A monarchy without a people." The country was the personal property of the sultans; they ran it, with tireless vigor, like a private estate and did not try to tone things down with a hypocritical flow of liberal proclamations. They were, however, as brave as they were proud; for proof of this, one has only to study their exploits against the Crusaders and the Mongols.

Under the iron rule of the Mamlūks, those prolific providers of generals and sultans who were supported by the unusual administrative ability of the jurists, the Moslem imperialism of Egypt dominated the Mediterranean. This was accomplished with the aid of European fleets, especially from Genoa, which were anxious to protect their commercial prosperity. The city of Cairo grew considerably, and splendid monuments sprang up in the streets of the old city and in the suburbs. Although we cannot pass over in silence the bloody struggles that took place in Cairo under their reign, we must admit that the Mamlūks had grandiose ideas which they carried out. After all, the period of the Italian Renaissance was in many respects just as painful. Just like their southern European contemporaries, who were engaged in never-ending feuds, the Mamlūks left behind them tangible and luxurious memorials, such as palaces, mosques, and sumptuous mausoleums. We must not forget Gobineau's famous statement: "In Cairo, the memory of the Mamlūks dominates everything; they accomplished so many things and founded so many solid and beautiful monuments. They alone were able to carve in marble and in stone the quantity of arabesques which cover with splendor the buildings of all of Asia. Once these former slaves, the Mamlūks, had their sabers at their sides and the power to command within their fists, they seem never to have had a petty thought; everything that they founded seemed to be without equal among Moslem works in the rest of the world."

The fifteenth century was especially saddened by the violent disagreements which brought the different factions of the Mamlūks to grips more and more frequently. Exterminating each other was not enough; they sacked the markets when the shops did not close on time. For the peaceful people of Cairo, the Mamlūk regime was a real nightmare; here was authority which oppresesd more than it protected. The artisans and shopkeepers never thought of organizing in order to free themselves from this yoke. In case of imminent danger, they contented themselves with hiding their expensive merchandise in safe places.

Life was hectic in Cairo because of the unbearable behavior of the military. This was hardly new from the time of the Fatimids on; yet the capital remained free of popular uprisings.

If we can try to draw conclusions from what has been

said, we can state that Cairo had a calm population which was not asked to interest itself in public affairs. Indeed this population, which had no more unity than it had determination, because of its excessive fragmentation, showed no desire to engage in public affairs. As elsewhere, we have soldiers, government officials, members of monasteries, merchants, and artisans. The members of the military, like the government, are not of Egyptian origin. They execute the orders of the sovereign who pays them, and use or abuse the authority granted them. The monarch and his militia, however, are not all-powerful and have to come to terms with another army, that of the scribes and the tax collectors, who hold the purse strings. In any event, these latter never brought down a regime or deposed a sultan through ill will or lack of co-operation. Never having been able to do without them, the sultans cunningly and intelligently considered Egypt as their own personal property which was to be managed by the scribes.

# 5
## Streets and Houses

A TRAVELER GAVE a résumé of the shortcomings which cannot be omitted if one is to describe medieval Cairo; he said: "The houses have neither the form nor the outward elegance of ours; the streets are narrow, unpaved, and crooked; immense, irregularly shaped areas, with no buildings to adorn them and no monument to mark and embellish their center, are, for the most part, vast pools of water during the overflowing of the Nile and fields or gardens when the river regains its bed. A crowd of men of many nations rushes and pushes through the streets and contends over the right of way with the Mamlūk's horse, the jurist's mule, camels which are used in place of vehicles, and donkeys which are the most usual mount."

Beyond Bāb al-Futūḥ, one still comes upon a street which has remained as it was during the Middle Ages. It runs north and south for almost four and one-half kilometers, from this southern gate to the Sayyida Nafisa shrine. This endless artery, the backbone of Cairo, was responsible for the city's unity. It has kept, at least in the northern part, the appearance it had in ancient times. Here it is lined by mysterious portals, there by shops, some of which are of such tiny dimensions that they look like large cases with one side removed so as to expose the interior. In front of each shop is a stone bench or little platform as long as the shop entrance and wide enough for a man to sit on. After opening his shop, the merchant places on the bench a mat, a rug, or a cushion and then sits down; when a customer comes, he has him sit next to him. In the evening, when the shopkeepers go home, the neighborhood is deserted.

The street has been laid out in an irregular manner; the houses seem to have been placed at random, without any attempt to set them in a row. Since each proprietor took whatever land he wanted to build on, the pedestrian now has to wind in and out. There is no lost space; shops and houses are built close to each other to the detriment of the street, just as in Egyptian villages where the houses are jammed together so that they will encroach as little as possible on land that can be cultivated. Although the general direction is rectilinear, the street itself winds almost imperceptibly. As a result, the horizon is always blocked. Since there are many mosques on this important street, there is always a minaret in the background.

It is said that a Moroccan sovereign scolded the inhabitants of his country when he found a street without a mosque. This complaint could not have been voiced in Cairo, where the streets were encumbered with sanctuaries. All along the streets there is one mosque after the other—two, three, four in a row, leaning against each other. Minarets embroidered with arabesques, intricately carved with the most varying fantasy, pierce the sky everywhere. Some are far off, some are near by and point to the sky above your head; wherever you look, as far as the eye can see, you discover them, and you seem always to be watched for a certain time by the one you have just passed. This is what amazed Seigneur d'Anglure in 1395.

"In this city, as we have truly been told, are found twelve thousand Saracen churches which are called *muscas*, in which they perform and recite their devotions. They are kept and maintained clean and are brightly lighted by beautiful lamps; yet, in these oratories there are no paintings, no images, and nothing that is not painted white; they are, all the same, well built of marble. There are some churches that are very big and very beautiful and seem to be like beautiful Christian churches."

One European traveler said that if the mosques of Cairo were assembled, they would form a city as large as Orleans!

Ibn Baṭṭuṭah, a keener observer than Ibn Khaldūn, wrote: "Cairo is the metropolis of the country, master of widespread regions and rich areas; it has attained the ultimate possible limits in the size of its population and is proud of its beauty and brilliance. It is the meeting place for travelers, a station for the weak and the poor. All kinds of men are found there, scholarly or ignorant, diligent or trivial, noble or plebian, unknown or famous. The number of inhabitants is so great that they seem to move in waves making the city look like a choppy sea. The city is almost too small to hold them in spite of its large area and its capacity."

The Europeans, too amazed by the density of the crowds, found it impossible to get the precise details. Simon Simeonis wrote in 1322: "In my opinion and in the absence of a better estimation, Cairo is twice as large as Paris and has four times the population; if I gave a larger figure, it would still be an understatement."

Toward the end of the century, Gucci di Dino was to say, without exaggerating: "Babylon is the ancient city. Cairo is the new city, founded and erected later. In both cities the population is countless, to such a point that it is estimated that they could supply six or eight hundred thousand armed men. They have easily three million souls, and it is estimated that more than seven hundred thousand men, women, and children are so poor that they never sleep in the same place two successive nights; they simply lie down on the ground or on benches where they happen to be."

For Simone Segoli, "the city of Cairo is more than twelve miles long and thirty miles in circumference. It has more than three hundred thousand inhabitants, more than fifty thousand of whom have neither a house nor a roof to shelter them. There are, in addition, more than ten thousand men who have no clothes on their backs and have only a small piece of cloth around their loins."

Frescobaldi thought that the population of Cairo was greater than that of all Tuscany and that there was one street in the city which alone had a greater population than Florence. In the first quarter of the fifteenth century, it is said that Cairo was fifteen miles long and five miles wide, and it was so densely populated that three or four people could hardly pass in a street without bumping into each other.

This was the situation even in the main streets. No one ever went for a walk in them; people went there only when they had to for their own affairs or to help out someone else. One could hardly walk without being pushed around by this swarming, jostling mob. It was this rush of pedestrians and horsemen, this flood of humanity, that gave the impression that the city was overpopulated.

What then can be said of the narrower streets? The Arab writers themselves complained about them, and travelers despaired of the confusing labyrinth, the inextricable network of narrow, dusty passages. Most of the alleys were short, very small, and narrower than those of Venice. Sometimes they were the length of two houses or a little more, so that the entire city was nothing but a jumble of houses.

Some of these passageways, in certain places, passed under the houses. We are reminded of this by a street which still today bears the name Under-the-Building Street. These passages through the buildings, known only by those who were thoroughly familiar with the city, remind us, except for the differences of level, of the *traboules* in Lyons. In addition, every twenty or thirty houses one ran into a gate which closed off the neighborhood. The purpose of the gates was not one of defense in time of war; they were simply there to prevent thieves from entering the houses at night or to keep one from finding his way out if he had been clever enough to get in. Sometimes the gate was closed in the middle of the day, and one was forced to go back and detour in order to reach one's destination. The job of the police, whose number had been reduced to a minimum, was made easier by these little streets which were blocked here and there.

The passageways were so narrow that two people could hardly walk abreast in them; a camel carrying a load was more of an obstruction than was a carriage in some streets of Paris. Doubtless, the passing of a camel loaded down with sugar cane forced even the proudest of passers-by to flatten himself against the wall. European travelers say that generally the streets were very dark, because, in certain places, the houses were so close to each other that the eaves overlapped and mats had been stretched from one roof to the other. The inconvenience of a narrow street, however, was more than made up for by its coolness. The narrowness of the streets caused a refreshing draft, and the tall houses cast a pleasant shadow on the passers-by. This was, then, a maze of little, narrow streets winding between walls with no windows and sometimes opening upon oddly shaped squares.

Simon Simeonis, at the beginning of the fourteenth century, neatly summed up the situation: "The city's dark, winding streets have many nooks and corners, are full of dust and other refuse, and are completely unpaved; the most important ones are so full of a barbaric crowd that one can go from one of them to the other only with the greatest difficulty."

At the end of the fifteenth century the impression was to be the same. Breydenbach wrote: "We visited the merchants' streets. The crowd reminded us of Saint Peter's in Rome during jubilee years. There is such a great number of buyers and sellers that one can hardly believe one's eyes; it is almost beyond belief. I do not think that there exists another city in the world today as populous, as large, as rich, and as powerful as Cairo. We went into one street, then another; then, going through an iron gate, we arrived at the most crowded intersections. Elbowing our way through masses of men, we saw one spot where the throng of people was beyond words."

We can imagine without much difficulty the crowd flowing out of the little adjacent streets and being swallowed up in the large one. A grumpy, imaginative traveler saw "people walking around with their arms dangling, without paying attention to anything as though they were waiting for the stroke of a wand which would turn them back into themselves and make their tired faces light up again with desire and hope." Let us not forget that the Egyptian population, especially in Cairo, was easygoing, gentle, noisily turbulent, and full of life. This human sea rolled on with good humor into its happy whirlpool, without wondering what era it was in or what the world was made of.

This last description is particularly evocative: "Three main streets cross the city; they are beautiful by comparison with the others which are narrow and winding, since each inhabitant built his house according to his own whim, blocking the passage and reducing streets to narrow, short alleys through which one can hardly pass, especially on market days. Often, too, houses are opened so that passages can go through them, but they are so dark that they could lend themselves to evil deeds. The most important one of these three longest streets crosses the length of the city. The market is held here every Monday and Thursday. Even though the street is rather wide, it is difficult to cross it on market days because of the large crowd, for it is here that everything in the way of food coming from the outside or from the city is brought to be sold. Another street opening into it is where the shops are located which sell the best wholesale merchandise."

The streets were encumbered by the benches which were placed in front of the shops, but that was not all. Hawkers set up shop on the ground with piles of bread and other food, in spite of the fact that the police were always after them. Circulation in the streets was also hindered by water carriers and by peddlers who offered the passers-by their shoddy goods or even food. They made known their presence by picturesque cries, just as one hears in all the cities of the world, "each one calling out his wares," as Seneca said about ancient Rome, "with personal inflections." These merchants did not enter the houses. The shutter of a latticework window, a moucharaby, would open and a pillow would be lowered on a length of cord. The merchandise would be raised into the home in this fashion. Barbers set up shop and shaved their customers' heads and necks outdoors. "Men walked along the streets with a sort of mirror tied to their chests and cried out, 'Who wants a shave?'" The artisans who worked in front of their shops must not be forgotten.

A certain number of porters were at the disposition of the customers; "these people are ready to do all sorts of errands for a modest fee." Here and there, there were bone setters to help those who had fainted or had been injured and to take care of fractures. *A Thousand and One Nights* uses the Zuweila gate area as the setting for an incident involving a pickpocket. Night patrols prevented disturbances and watched out for thieves. Each night the officer of the watch took off on a set route; he was preceded by a torch bearer and surrounded by police officers, water carriers, and wreckers who all had their duties in fighting fire which might break out in the night. Anyone who engaged in a fist fight or who was caught stealing was arrested.

It is possible, in view of their periodic renewal, that statutes concerning the streets were not always strictly applied, but they prove, nevertheless, that the authorities did not remain inactive. No shipment of straw or of firewood was permitted to go through the main street; a groom was not allowed to lead a horse down this street; water carriers had to cover their goatskin bottles in order not to splash passers-by; shopkeepers were obliged to keep a jar full of water handy to fight fires. These precautions were really rather childish, just as it was of no great help, in 1014, to have removed the porch roofs and the benches in order to eliminate evident fire hazards and to clear obstacles from the path of the fire fighters. Through sheer good fortune, disasters were rather rare. There were, however, serious fires in 1321 and especially in 1350. All the water carriers were mobilized and all the carpenters were called up to destroy whatever was in the immediate path of the fire, to no avail. The fire lasted for one whole month in 1350.

During the night, shopkeepers were supposed to hang

lanterns in front of their stores. Yet when Breydenbach entered the city, after having left Matariya in 1483, he indicated that he "had a long walk in the dark." Five years later, according to the Italian rabbi Da Bertinoro, "one could go out in Cairo at night as well as during the day, because all the streets are lighted by torches." Trevisano stated quite precisely that it was "customary in Cairo, as a security measure, to keep a lamp burning at the door of one house in every group of four or five." But this measure was not strictly carried out, for during the reign of the half-mad son of Qāyit Bey, "every night after the evening prayer, he himself made the rounds in the streets as he was preceded by two globe-shaped lanterns and four torches. Ahead of him walked several black slaves. If he passed in front of a shop that did not have a lantern, he had the shop nailed shut as he remained there to supervise the operation." During Ramaḍān many lamps lit up the towers of the mosques, and one was struck by the sight of thousands of shining towers, each one of them lighted by three rows made up of a countless number of lamps. "Because of these lights, the city shone as brightly as though it were in the middle of the day."

From time to time the government became concerned with the cleanliness of the capital; this probably happened more frequently than the chronicles indicate. We know that at the end of the fourteenth century the shopkeepers were forced to refinish the fronts of their stores. In May, 1477, an order was given to widen the avenues, the streets, and the alleys. The demolition was ordered, in the streets and the market places, of all constructions without legal title, such as many buildings of income property, porch roofs, balconies, and benches. The widening of the streets was greatly advantageous, but many individuals suffered serious losses because of the disappearance of their property and their shops. The city of Cairo was stirred up over the destruction of these buildings, especially those that were on the main arteries, and the decree was generally unpopular.

Yet this did not discourage the government, which went on from there to repair the façades and the doors of the mosques, to clean their marble, and to whiten their walls. There was an order given to wash the shops and to resurface the front of buildings facing the streets. An inspector of streets was appointed whose duty it was to get the proprietors moving and to hurry along the resurfacing and the painting. Our Arab chronicler adds that, as a result, the city became as beautiful as it had been at the time of its founding and as resplendent as a bride when she unveils her face before her husband. At the same time, work was begun at Bāb Zuweila to raise the roadbed to the level of the surrounding streets.

Despite his lyricism, the historian who gives us those details does not always hide his ill humor. He tells us that in 1498 it was proclaimed by order of the sultan that shops facing the streets and the market places were to be painted white and decorated with colors. Because of this, the shopkeepers had enormous expenses. Our writer blames this situation on the instigation of individuals of the lowest class and on schemers who surrounded the sovereign.

In November, 1503, a proclamation from the sultan ordered all shopkeepers to dig out the streets in order to lower them by one cubit, since their level had risen considerably. Those concerned were invited to complete this task without too much delay; this caused a good deal of consternation, since day laborers to carry off the earth could not be found because of the great demand.

Bad weather was rare in Cairo, and the installation of rain

gutters over certain Fatimid doors indicates that the archi-
tects were of foreign origin. Yet there were sometimes tor-
rential rains which flooded the market places and the streets.
Flaubert wrote: "It rained all week. Twice we ventured forth
in our big boots into the streets of Cairo, which were full
of lakes of mud. The poor Arabs floundered around in it up
to their knees and shivered. Business is at a halt; the bazars
are closed and look sad and cold. Some of the houses are
collapsing under the rain. Ashes and rubbish are thrown on
the mud in order to dry it up; this is how the level of the
land is gradually raised."

Certainly there were men hired to keep the streets of the
city clean, but they also had alert assistants to help them. A
traveler wrote: "In the streets of Cairo there are so many
kites that it is almost unbelievable. They fly around the city
as freely as hens, so much so that I have often seen them eat
the meat right off the heads of those who were carrying it
through the city. Sometimes they fly and snatch the meat
from their hands. No one would dare hurt them, because
they eat decaying carcasses and other refuse. After the Nile
has overflowed and has regained its natural course, it leaves
behind a great deal of filth; when it is at its height, dead
animals, fish, and snakes come down the main streets, but
there is so great a number of these nasty birds that they
devour everything immediately."

A sixteenth-century traveler tells us: "It is not lawful to
chase or kill these birds, because they clean the Nile of its
filth and also the city, which could not be kept clean because
of its size."

\*　　\*　　\*

We have seen the inhabitants of Cairo walk about in the
dense crowds. Just as in our day, there must have been

clusters of people at the entrance to the hospitals and the prisons. We should not forget the unfortunate ones gathered around the public scribes, who existed even in modern times. If the Arab authors neglected to call our attention to this group, it is because they were so accustomed to it. The scribes, who must have been very numerous, set up shop in the open air and blocked the entrances to public and administrative buildings.

"Here is a shop of severe appeerence that stands out from its neighboring shops. On several small boards there are merely some books and some sheets of paper. An attentive man, with an ink pot placed in front of him, writes leaning on his knees; another person leaning toward him answers his questions. The scribe is a man worth consulting, one should get his advice in all matters which are a little difficult in this life."

It has been said: "It is in the old neighborhoods that people feel more or less at home and at ease with each other. They like the animation and the color of the narrow streets; they enjoy the tiny shops and this life in an ant-hill. One would be almost tempted to say that this is necessary for their happiness. What is striking in these neighborhoods is the life outdoors, the cheerful readiness for conversation, the good-natured, rarely vulgar familiarity, and an enjoyment of life that lights up their faces."

With rare exception, the nobles and others who had a certain degree of prestige always rode horses in the streets. The women rode donkeys, and nothing was funnier than seeing them perched astride these little trotting animals. Merchants who were in a hurry to transact their business rode donkeys, too.

The donkey has almost disappeared today, like some antediluvian animal, but in the Middle Ages there were twenty thousand donkeys for rent in the city. They stood at the inter-section of streets and waited patiently for customers who wanted to ride them within or outside the city. A traveler wrote that he need only say that there were as many available as there were sedan-chairs in Naples, gondolas in Venice, or carriages in Rome. What is most remarkable is that each animal had its driver, a man or child who pricked the donkey from behind to keep it moving, so that there was always a line of men and animals running along the streets. We are told that it was truly amusing to see this great number of gentle, pretty donkeys which were decorated, properly decked out in beautiful silk blankets, and had their ears, manes, and tails painted yellow.

The pert trot of the donkey was contrasted with the haughty, scornful bearing of the camel, "that strange animal that hops about like a turkey and swings its neck like a swan." There were interminable processions of solemnly lurching camels who refused to move except in a straight line, as though the straightness of the streets depended upon them. As a matter of fact, the standard width of the main streets was the width of two camels walking abreast with loads of straw. We know from others that a single camel loaded with firewood—that is, a width of nine cubits—could pass down these streets.

A curious accident which occurred in September, 1508, shows how dangerous this could be. Soon after nightfall, a peasant led through the streets two camels carrying flax. A shopkeeper's lantern set the flax on fire, and the panic-stricken camels rushed into the crowd, trampled pedestrians, and caused a large number of deaths. Finally the camels fell to the ground.

Almost all of the travelers have observed that there was no need for streets which could accommodate vehicles drawn by animals. One of them tells us: "You should know that, with some rare exceptions, there is no place in Egypt where carts and vehicles are used, as in the western countries. All objects which cannot be loaded on ships or camels are transported on the backs of donkeys or oxen."

From time to time one did see in Cairo other means of transportation, but these cases were so exceptional that the chroniclers made a point of them. Thus, in 1369 two marble columns were transported by means of rollers and winches. The popular poets found this a subject for their wit, and designs depicting this scene were embroidered on scarves. Several years later stones were extracted from the Muqaṭṭam quarries and placed in wagons drawn by oxen; from then on these materials were called the "carted stones." In May, 1512, the sultan ordered that cannons that had just been manufactured be transported to the desert north of Cairo where they could be tested. They were placed in ox-drawn wagons. Passing between the shops on the street running from the Citadel to the mosque of Ibn Ṭūlūn proved to be quite troublesome and was accomplished with enormous difficulty. Finally the ground gave way; a large artillery piece fell into an underground passage, and it took a great amount of effort to get it out.

Both heat and dust had to be fought in these streets. Many unpaved passageways had to be sprinkled twice a day. We are told that in places that were not sprinkled the dust rose as thick as smoke, and it was hard to tell if it was just dust or a fire.

The city of Cairo itself was rather far from the Nile, and the water problem took up the time of a considerable number of men and animals. Ibn Baṭṭūṭah assures us that Cairo claimed 12,000 water carriers who used camels and 30,000 muleteers. Frescobaldi estimates at 130,000 the number of camels and other animals used to deliver water throughout the city. At the beginning of the sixteenth century Trevisano notes that 15,000 camels went to the Nile twice a day to get water for the city's needs. These animals were probably not very well treated. *A Thousand and One Nights* tries to move us to pity with the story of the lamentations of a donkey who has fled the society of men to avoid becoming a water carrier.

It was necessary to provide each lodging with water, supply the public baths, fill the drinking troughs set up for animals, and replenish the porous, earthen vases placed on tripods and covered with a board on which was kept a drinking cup. In the streets there were men who carried, hanging from their necks, goatskin bottles with cloth tubes and who sold to the passer-by all the water he wished to drink, served in silver or copper cups. Some of these men were hired by the rich, who wished to offer this essential commodity as charity to the poor.

The itinerant water carriers had to use leather bottles tanned by the bark of the acacia. This process assured durability. Leather made of mule-skin and dirty or worm-eaten leather could not be used. The carriers had to get their water in the Nile far from all impurities. They especially went upriver from the sewers of the bathhouses or a long distance downstream. When a carrier used a new goatskin bottle, he was not, for some time, to deliver water in it for household consumption; he sold his water to mills, wine presses, or brick factories. Animals bearing water bottles had to wear around their necks bells or collars made of iron or copper strips so that, in the market places, the blind, the absent-minded, and the young could be warned of their approach.

We are told that there were many itinerant merchants who, as was the custom of their country, sold chicks by weight and not by number. All the travelers were amazed to find that in Egypt eggs were hatched "without any help from the hens." They tell us that these people had a process for hatching chicks. They put one thousand or more eggs together in ovens containing several shelves; the top shelf had a hole in it. A low fire was kept burning under this piece of equipment. After seven days masses of chicks began hatching. They were gathered up in containers and, when sold, were weighted by a bottomless instrument which was put into the customer's basket. This measuring device was filled with chicks, and, when it could hold no more, it was removed. The pilgrim Breydenbach became quite philosophical about this: "Hatched without the help of a mother, they are sent like sheep into the fields with a shepherd or they are sold in the market place. What is unbelievable, yet really true, is that these animals, born through the art and industry of man, are more docile than those born following their natural laws. They follow men just as ordinary chicks follow their mother."

\*     \*     \*

The European travelers gave contradictory descriptions of the houses of the city. This is explained by the fact that some accounts depicted rich and official residences while others described more modest homes, which were poor, low, flat, and thatch roofed. The wealthier homes were certainly less well built than those in Europe. They sometimes had four or five stories; the lower part of the building was made of cut stone or brick, the upper part of very light wood, palm fronds, reeds, and earth. Instead of roofs, they had terraces where the inhabitants cooled off in the evening and where some persons even slept in the summer.

The houses had very simple façades and bare walls with no decorations. Their main ornament facing the street was the moucharabies, trellises which projected from the outside walls and which were made up of an infinite number of small pieces of carved wood, arranged and put together so as to make the most varied designs. In a more practical way, these moucharabies "served to satisfy the curiosity of those who were indoors and could not be penetrated by the indiscretion of those who were outdoors." The medieval house, therefore, remained mysterious and hermetic. It was said that it tried, in this way, to hide its opulence, but one can think of a more natural reason for this exterior simplicity. If private homes did not have rich façades, it was merely because they were useless in view of the narrowness of the streets. It would have been impossible to back away far enough to enjoy them.

The homes belonging to important people were very humble, ordinary, and almost grim looking on the outside, but inside they were of unequaled elegance and richness. They were, as one traveler remarked, "the house of God and the gates of heaven." These homes were decorated with very fine, varied paintings of admirable, rich design and with marble and other colored stones. It seems that in the Orient beauty was supposed to remain hidden, just as women were formerly veiled and, even earlier, mummies were wrapped in strips of cloth.

The reception room was paved with varicolored marble, inlaid to form flowers or other decorations, in the midst of which sprang one or two jets of water which were kept going day and night during the entire summer. Around this vast pool of water were placed here and there vases filled with flowers of the season. This jet of running water could be considered an indispensable part of the wealthy home; it was almost the equivalent of the hearth in the West. The floor was covered with mats, if only at both ends where there were divans, platforms raised two and one-half feet covered with precious Persian rugs, silk and gold cushions, or a fine colored cloth with gold fringes. Here the people sat tailor fashion, with their legs crossed under them.

The house in which Jehan Thenaud lived, at the beginning of the sixteenth century, included "six or seven beautiful rooms paved with marble, porphyry, serpentine, and other rich stones set with exceptional art, with walls encrusted with the same materials, painted with gold, blue, and rich colors; the workmanship always surpassed the materials. In these rooms there were fountains through which ran both hot and cold water brought by hidden pipes. Near here were numerous trees and plants bearing fruit such as lemons, limes, pumpkins, oranges, apricots, cassia, and apples. Each evening and morning, these gardens are sprinkled with water brought from the Nile by oxen and horses."

The walls were generally covered with marble to a height of ten or twelve feet; above this was a magnificent cornice, sometimes of gilded bronze set with very fine porcelain. The ceiling consisted of coffers and jutting rafters.

Our travelers were impressed by the procedures used to fight the heat of the summer. In addition to the pools of water, a type of ventilating shaft opened toward the north and connected with very narrow passages through which the air flowed rapidly to mingle with the coolness created by the marble and the water.

The Cairo house received its light from the interior court

and not at all from the street. We can almost say that the house was built from the inside out and that the owner, afterwards, blocked out the street. These homes were pleasant enough and far enough from the noises of the town to permit the residents to escape from their business worries and from the bustle of the city and to have a few hours of peace. It was in these shut-up houses that one could best feel safe, isolated from tribulations, and removed from daily life. One could meditate at leisure near the pool in the central court as one listened to the murmur of the fountain and the song of the birds.

The houses did not contain furniture like ours. First of all, there was no kitchen; all the travelers state that food was brought in from the outside. It was brought cooked and prepared from caterers who were found throughout the city. There were no removable chairs; the people sat on benches covered with mats and cushions. There was no bedding, in our sense of the word; a mat sufficed. This led Gobineau to say: "What would have appeared to be austerity elsewhere was Sybaritism here." The water jars were kept in a little alcove. The amount of copperware, such as basins, ewers, and cups, depended upon the wealth of the owner. There were many chests full of trinkets, porcelain, precious rugs, and cushions covered with cloth made of gold and silver thread. The capital of these homeowners consisted of rich cloth. This is proved by the fact that in troubled times the cloth was the first thing to be put in a safe place.

The general plan was to protect the intimacy of the harem and to keep family life hidden from the eyes of strangers. Because of the zigzagging entrance, the door could be left open as a symbol of hospitality, but the passer-by could not rush into the house. This winding vestibule led to the central court. The most essential part of the house was the salon reserved for men.

\* \* \*

It is obvious that houses were planned so that women could remain cloistered. But it would be incorrect to believe that women were deprived of all freedom. Tales from this part of the world have perhaps exaggerated many other things, but they have been quite explicit in telling of feminine intrigues. Women could go out; they went to the baths, for example, and that was no minor affair. They were present at anniversaries, family celebrations, weddings, and births; they went on pilgrimages and thronged to the well-known shrines. Moreover, from the way in which Cairo homes were arranged and furnished, it would be difficult to imagine that the heads of households had not considered and consulted their wives. The luxury, wealth, and elegance of the home and the beauty of the interior flower gardens were all for the benefit of the women.

Women must have had a good deal of freedom if one is to judge by the restrictions that the strict moralists felt called upon to write. They thought that women should not visit the cemeteries, nor should they live in houses facing the canal or the ponds because of the scenes that they might witness. For the same reason, women should not travel in boats, and they should not be present at the mahmal procession.

In accordance with these austere principles, women should go out only when necessary; they should be dressed in their oldest clothes and should be completely covered by a cloak reaching the ground. They should not wear their most beautiful dresses and walk proudly down the streets. It was considered scandalous for women to be found in the shops of cloth merchants and jewelers or to speak smilingly to them. The presence of women in the market places of Cairo was so common that a jurist complained that non-Moslem women, too richly dressed, were greeted by merchants who thought they were Moslems. In *A Thousand and One Nights* most of the little romances take place in the cloth market.

Theoretically, there would have been only three reasons for a woman to leave home: to go to the home of her new husband, to attend the funeral of her parents, and to be buried at the time of her own death. These rather severe theorists really had no illusions; they knew that they were preaching in the desert, and they readily admitted that women went out each week to visit the tombs of Ḥusain and Nafisa.

Here is how Frescobaldi saw them: "The clothing of the women is generally of finely woven cloth, and what they wear underneath is made of buckram or, among the richest, of fine Alexandrian linen. Some women wear a short cotton garment that reaches the knees, but in that case they wear a type of Roman coat over it. They are veiled and hidden so that only their eyes can be seen; the most distinguished among them wear in front of their eyes a coarsely woven piece of black muslin which, while preventing them from being seen, permits them to see others perfectly well. On their feet they have short, white boots, and their legs are covered with stockings and leggings that come down to their heels. The ends of these leggings are decorated, according to the lady's station, with silk, gold, silver, stones, or pearls embroidered into the cloth."

Trevisano adds: "No part of their body is seen, except their hands, and even that is rare. They all wear white clothes and sit astride little donkeys as they ride through the city. Some of the women have painted hands and red-tinted nails. They spend a great deal of money in the bazars on silks and perfumes."

# 6

## *Sanctuaries and Markets*

As IN ALL EASTERN CITIES the *sūqs*, or market places, stretched on endlessly. An Arab author states: "The casbah is the vastest of all the markets of Egypt. From what I have heard the older men say, there were twelve thousand shops on this boulevard, and they stretched from the artery leading to the beginning of Ḥusainiyya, at the edge of the sand plain, up to the Nafisa mausoleum. When one judges the distance that separates these two points, one cannot deny the accuracy of this information. As a matter of fact, I walked the whole length of this area and found it covered with shops full of food, drink, and all sorts of merchandise wonderful to behold, displayed to enchant the eye, and defying all statistics. I am not even going to talk about the number of customers. All the people I approached outdid each other in boasting of the superiority of Egypt over other countries. They said that the trash that was thrown into the rubbish heaps and dumps of Cairo each day was worth a thousand gold dinars. They were referring to the utensils used by the milk merchants, the cheese dealers, and the food tradesmen. These are red, earthen vessels into which milk and cheese are put or in which the poor eat their food in the cook-shops. They were thinking, too, of the string used by the cheese merchants, the wicker trays placed between the cheese and its container, the paper utilized by the druggists, and the cord for tying up sacks in which were put foodstuff such as grain and condiments. For once this food was brought home from the market

93

and was put away, the wrappings were thrown out in the trash."

Merchants piled loaves of bread and other food items on the ground. Very often the magistrates received appeals to prevent these people from setting up shop in the market places, since they blocked the narrow streets and hurt the business of the shopkeepers.

Beyond the Bāb al-Futūḥ ran the wall of the Ḥakim mosque, whose quadrangular towers harmonized perfectly with the surrounding ramparts. This mosque, with its squat pillars, makes one think of the general plan of the Ibn Ṭūlūn mosque. Marilhat gives us a picture of the mosque "with its pathetic, gilded ruins, its arcades violently thrust up against the cloudless sky, its upright, mutilated pillars, and with a caravan resting in the debris as though overcome with fatigue caused by the battle between shade and sunlight." A divine curse seems to have weighed upon the shrine of that strange caliph, that Caligula of Moslem history, who dared proclaim himself god. The building, along with its court, has taken on the appearance of a victim condemned to dust.

Inside the Bāb al-Futūḥ there were the shops of butchers, grain and vegetable dealers, and other merchants of that type. This was the best known and the most frequented of all the markets in Cairo. People came from everywhere in the country to buy all kinds of vegetables and all types of meat: mutton, beef, kid. The butchers wrapped the meat in banana leaves.

Not far from there was located a market which dealt in riding saddles for camels and everything else that was needed to equip them. People went there from all over Egypt, especially just before the pilgrimage season. Anyone who wanted to fit out one hundred camels or more in a single day and who had had trouble doing so elsewhere came here because of the great quantitiy of equipment in the shops or in the merchants' stockrooms.

From there to the al-Aqmar mosque food was sold: raw or cooked meat, bread, oil, cheese, milk, vegetables, and various spices. There were a great number of shops where fried food or roasts could be bought day or night. There were itinerant cooks not only at this central point but throughout the city. The people of Cairo rarely prepared their meals at home; they bought them already cooked from caterers or chefs who were found throughout the city and who specialized in this work. It is said that there were from ten to twelve thousand cooks who wandered up and down the streets of the city, carrying on their heads lighted stoves, with pots boiling, or meat roasting on spits, as they offered those around them their simmering wares. Frescobaldi adds that the cooks prepared their food in beautiful copper-plated caldrons. We are told that the city people often sat and ate in the street; they spread a skin on the ground, placed a bowl containing their food on it, and gathered around squatting on their heels or sitting cross-legged. Thus, the people lived on what they bought at these kitchens where there was a plentiful supply of meat, especially lamb, chickens, geese, and an even greater quantity of rice and fritters prepared in oil. Other details inform us that "the cooks chop up the meat into little pieces and put it on spits, as we do thrushes, and then they put it into ovens which are open on top; the meat is cooked in an instant. Sometimes they cook a whole sheep, and after it is done, a man carries it on his shoulders, puts a table on his head, and goes through the streets crying, 'Who wants to eat meat?' Because they have no inns, strangers are obliged to eat wherever they happen to be."

On the left, lower down, can be seen the charmingly melancholy, narrow façade of the al-Aqmar mosque. Let us stop and consider this exquisite monument. It does not seem to be much, compared to the colossal gates at the entrance to the city or the majestic buildings of the Mamlūks which we shall soon see. But we have more than one reason for admiring it. Here the archaeologist can solve several problems concerning the development of Islamic decoration. But for the artist it is a work of sober eloquence and charming simplicity. This jewel is one of the most beautiful results of the work of the Fatimid builders.

Near this sanctuary was the candlemakers' market. There could be seen tapers for lanterns, torches for the sergeants of the watch, and candles of respectable size to be used in processions. Doubtless they no longer made the candles that used to be placed on the mules' rumps in the time of the Ikhshidids. (The mule drivers had to turn around constantly to check on the position of the candles.) The shops were open until late into the night and became the meeting place of the prostitutes, who, as a result, were called the candlemakers' ribald women. They wore loud clothes so that they could be recognized.

Immediately to the northeast of this area, toward the Bāb al-Naṣr gate, swarmed the cloth merchants and their associated artisans, such as weavers, fullers, dyers, darners, tailors, launderers, pressers, and designers—in other words, all those who were in the clothing trade. Other more original specialists were near by, including those who made curious wooden locks that amazed European travelers. One of them says: "The locks and the keys are just made of wood, even those for the gates of the city. The key is a piece of wood an eighth of an ell long, an inch wide, and as thick as a little finger; fixed into the end there are about six or eight pins made of brass wire or even wood, about one inch high. These pins, coming in contact with others which are inside the lock, remove them, and the lock opens."

It was near there, in the fourteenth century, that the slave market was found. It was later moved to the Khan al-Khalili, whose name became famous, and was to be described by travelers from the sixteenth century on. Men and women, who were for sale, were displayed there. Most of them wore nothing but a cloth around their loins. The customers examined all parts of their bodies to make sure that they were in good health, just as one does when buying horses. "They handled the slaves a great deal. Hands checked the muscles of a leg, the fineness of the skin, the firmness of a taut breast, the size of a virile fist." There were Turkish, Greek, Circassian, Georgian, and Abyssinian women. We can almost hear the dealer's patter recited in a bantering voice as it is given us in *A Thousand and One Nights*: "Rich merchants, not everything that is round is a nut, not everything that is long is a banana, not everything that is red is flesh, not everything that is brown is a date. Merchant, how much do you offer for this unique pearl, who is worth more than all your fortunes combined? Let's have the opening bids!"

Beyond the al-Aqmar mosque, toward the south, was the rather vast poultry and bird market; chickens and geese in unbelievable numbers were sold here. Some shops sold sparrows, which children bought so that they could set them free. One could also buy, cage and all, songbirds, turtledoves, blackbirds, parrots, quails, and nightingales.

From there one came to one of the busiest and most pleasant parts of Cairo, the street of Bain al-Qaṣreyn, "Between the Two Palaces," a name that goes back to the Fatimid period.

97

It was at that time a large area, free of all construction, which could hold ten thousand troops, both cavalrymen and foot soldiers. It was there that military parades and some reviews took place. After the fall of the dynasty, when the uninhabited palaces were occupied by the Ayyūbid princes and officers, the site served as a daily food market for various types of meat, pastries, fruit, and other such items. It was still a pleasant spot where notables and other important people liked to stroll at night to be entertained or to look at the vast profusion of light cast by lamps and chandeliers. Groups gathered to listen to biographical or historical recitations or to watch the various performances.

Later a veritable museum of architecture, a collection of splendid monuments, was to be found there. First there is the sultan Barkuk's school whose high walls and squat minaret catches the eye. Then there is the group of buildings erected by Qalāwun and his son Mohammed one hundred years earlier. A strange portal interests us, and we remember that it is the door of a Frankish church brought back from Palestine; this is not a war trophy but rather the choice of a man of good taste. Toward the east, a little to one side, there is the mausoleum of al-Malik al-Ṣālih Ayyūb, St. Louis' adversary.

These monuments of different periods, styles, and functions, standing side by side, do not at all clash with each other. They even create a type of harmony. This is certainly because of the light and the broken lines which make things stand out immediately. This is a sublime and stirring group of historical monuments. The four buildings forming the western façade are decorated with bands of inscriptions which give the visitor a feeling of the mystery of Arabic calligraphy.

At the beginning of the Mamlūk period the arms market, where bows, arrows, and coats of mail were bought, was situated here. This market was later moved near the Citadel.

Since that was just about the central point of the *sūqs*, in the north-south axis, there were a great number of money changers who had their shops in the area. Not far off were the benches of the Bazar of the Little Cages where jewels were on display. These little cages were made of iron latticework and held ring settings, seals, bracelets and foot rings.

As one went on, one found comb merchants, book dealers, and candy makers who had great supplies of pistachio nuts, almonds, and raisins. Near by the manufacturers of spurs displayed everything from their simplest articles made of iron to the most luxurious ones made of silver or of solid gold. They also dealt in all the metal parts of the harness. Close at hand was the harness makers' bazar where one could see reins, bridles, and especially saddles made of leather dyed in all colors, either plain or encrusted with silver and gold. Then came the cloth merchants' shops where imported materials were sold. These were used for draperies, cushions, saddle blankets, and more and more for the clothing of the middle class during the fifteenth century.

We then come to the monuments of the sultan Ghūri, which indicate the taste of an upstart, if a Mamlūk can be called one. His works give evidence of a style belonging to a degenerate nobility. There are poor imitations surviving from an inspired period. This art, which is a little too finicky and theatrical, came close to being bound by the rules of a school. It could be said in retrospect that Ghūri's artisans overdid things in trying to leave us evidence of a style which was about to disappear. As perfect as the decoration may be technically, it is merely a continuation of what has been done before, with no personality of its own. The undeniable, but conventional, ability of the artists shows more knowledge of technique than it does of inventive genius. We are, for example, more amused than moved by the frail, rather comic aspect of epigraphy which is neither serious nor robust. This work of lesser artists can be defined as a well-done assignment turned in by a good pupil. The artists of this period tend to add to an already ornate decoration without understanding the art of sacrificing for the sake of simplification.

Not far from there, in the vicinity of the al-Azhar mosque, were found the fur merchants who sold expensive sable, lynx, ermine, and squirrel furs. These were used at first by the officers of the sultans entourage and by high officials, and later, at the end of the fourteenth century, by ladies of the wealthy class.

In this area was the woodworkers' market. Cradles were sold in their shops. The center of the moucharaby industry was found here. These artisans, who used their toes to help them in their work, could hardly have executed the same movements with as much precision and speed had they used their hands.

Beyond the site where Ghūri's monuments were to be erected in the early part of the sixteenth century was the flourishing fourteenth-century market where inlaid copper articles were made. These admirable vessels inlaid with gold and silver consisted of trays, basins, ewers, small boxes, and perfume burners. There was hardly a house in Cairo or Old Cairo that did not have an inlaid copper article of some kind. But during the fifteenth century these artisans had already almost completely disappeared.

By this time the twin minarets had already been perched with perfect artistry above the Zuweila gate, the southern limit of the Fatimid city. These were part of the mosque built early in the fifteenth century by the sultan al-Malik Mū'ayyad. We shall soon have occasion to walk along its curious merlons.

Bāb Zuweila, during the Mamlūk period, was the sovereigns' entrance to the city, since they came from the direction of the Citadel. It was also here that the bodies of important criminals, especially prisoners of war, were left hanging as an example to the public. It was similar to the Rue de l'Estrapade in Paris, where the gallows were erected.

In the vicinity there were cooked-food vendors and especially candy makers whose specialties were multicolored sweets and sugar dolls. The sale of cakes in the form of people, animals, horses, lions, and cats scandalized Moslem puritans. Maqrīzi saw a plate on which were dried fruit and red potsherds containing milk and various kinds of cheese; between the potsherds there was an arrangement of cucumbers and bananas. All of this was made of sugar. All sorts of delicacies were sold here. In another near-by market one could purchase musical instruments such as guitars and lutes. This was the meeting place of libertines and other unsavory characters.

Travelers had a great deal to say about the wealth of the inhabitants of Cairo. One of them stated with a certain amount of lyricism: "If I were to describe the wealth of the city, this book would not suffice. If it were possible to gather together the cities of Rome, Milan, Padua, Florence and still four others, I swear that they could not all contain half of the wealth of Cairo." It was a city of immense commercial traffic, since merchandise flowed to it from the East Indies, Ethiopia, the Barbary Coast, Asia Minor, and Europe. There were great quantities of silk, purple dyes, brilliant diamonds, precious stones, beautifully designed stained glass which was manufactured in Damascus at that time, and gold, silver, and bronze vases sculptured in the Saracen fashion with incomparable art. There was an abundance of various kinds of spices. It should be said too that in this city, as in all of Egypt, roses, as well as other flowers, and fruit could be found in all seasons at reasonable prices.

"In the different sections of the city there are several markets or public places established for commercial purposes; these are called bazars, and each one is particularly set aside for a certain type of merchandise. Some of them deal in things brought by caravans from Ethiopia and usually handle drugs, parrots, and gold dust. Precious stones, cloth, fine linens, and many other products all have their separate bazars, and when one wants to buy something, one has only to find out which bazar sells it and how richly supplied it is. Some are covered and others are not. The rules governing these markets seemed to everyone to be among the best in Cairo. In each of these markets, there is usually a great gathering of people, for they find it advantageous to deal together here just as in the Palais in Paris, the Bourse in Antwerp, or the Exchange in Lyons."

Simone Segoli says: "There is in the city a great abundance of merchandise of all kinds, especially spices of all sorts which come from the two Indies across the Ocean and through the Red Sea and are unloaded at Tor, which is about fifteen miles from the foot of Mount Sinai. There is also an abundance of sugar as white as snow and as hard as stone; it is the best sugar in the world. After having been unloaded at this port, the merchandise is carried on camel back through the desert to Cairo. This is a thirteen day trip during which neither house nor roof is encountered and only the mountain and the sandy plain covered with stones and gravel are seen."

Maqrīzi took pleasure in speaking at great length of the prosperity of the markets of Cairo, but each of his statements ends with bitter reflections calling attention to the disappearance of most of the shops. The historian complained of the mournful sight offered in his time, the middle of the fifteenth century, by these markets which had become as sad "as a lonely post in the middle of a deep hole." It is true that we notice in the fifteenth century the decadence of all artistic industries and the complete disappearance of some of them, such as the manufacture of enameled glass and inlaid copper. In any event, it might be well to repeat the still enthusiastic description by Leo Africanus during the first quarter of the sixteenth century:

"The city is well provided with artisans and merchants. They are especially found in a street which goes from Bāb al-Naṣr to the Zuweila gate. This is where most of the nobles of Cairo are found. There are in this street several schools which are admired because of their size, their height, and their decorations. There are also to be seen several spacious and very beautiful temples. There are also several bathhouses built with great architectural art.

"A section called Bain al-Qaṣreyn contains shops where cooked meat is sold; there are about sixty of them in all supplied with tin dishes. In others water is prepared with all kinds of flowers. This water has a very fine taste; therefore, the nobles drink it. Those who sell it keep it in glass bottles or in tin ones which are very artistically decorated. After that there are other shops where are sold very nicely presented sweets, different from those usually sold in Europe. There are two kinds: those made of honey and those made of sugar. Then come the fruit dealers who sell the fruits of

Syria, such as pears, quinces, and pomegranates, which do not grow in Egypt. Interspersed among these shops are others where fritters, fried eggs, and fried cheese are sold. Near these shops is found a neighborhood occupied by artisans practicing noble trades. Farther along is the new school built by the sultan Ghūri. Beyond the school are the cloth fonduks, and each fonduk contains a great number of shops. In the first fonduk foreign cloth of the best quality is sold, such as that which comes from Baalbek, an extremely fine cotton material, and the cloth from Mosul which is admired for its fine quality and its strength. All the important and distinguished people use it to make their shirts and the veils which they wear on their turbans. Then come the fonduks where the most beautiful Italian cloth, such as damask satin, velvet, taffeta, and brocade is sold. I can assure you that I have not seen any to equal them in Italy where they are made. Farther on are the fonduks for woolens, which also come from all the countries of Europe: cloth from Venice, Majorca, and the Marches. Still farther on, camlet cloth is sold. Little by little, one gets to the Zuweila gate, where there is also a great number of artisans. Near this street is seen a fonduk called Khan al-Khalili, where the Persian merchants stay. This fonduk looks like a great lord's palace; it is very high, very solid, and has three floors. On the ground floor are the rooms where the merchants receive their customers and sell merchandise of great value. Only merchants who are very wealthy have a counter in this fonduk. Their merchandise consists of spices, precious stones, and cloth from India, such as crepe.

"On the other side of the main street, there is a section where are found perfume merchants who deal in civet, musk, amber, and benzoin. These products are found in such abundance that if anyone wants to buy one ounce of musk from a merchant, he is shown one hundred pounds of it. This is amazing. The area where beautiful glazed paper is sold borders this same main street. The merchants who sell this paper also sell precious stones. A crier carries them from shop to shop announcing what has been bid for them.

"Still on this same street there is a section where gold-smiths are found; they are Jews between whose hands great fortunes pass. In another section dealers in second-hand merchandise have set up shop. They sell a great deal of top quality cloth which has been turned over to them by towns-people and people of high rank. Here there are no short-coats, overcoats, or veils, but rather admirable pieces of cloth of unbelievable value."

Leo Africanus adds certain details which seem to give evidence of an embryonic corporate organization: "When it happens that one of the artisans turns out a beautiful, ingenious piece of work which has never before been seen, he is dressed in a brocaded coat, taken from shop to shop, accompanied by musicians in a sort of triumphal walk, and everyone gives him money. I saw a man in Cairo who had received one of these triumphal honors for having made a chain for a flea which he kept chained on a piece of paper. One of his friends exhibited it and collected the money. I also saw a feat of strength performed by one of those water-carriers who walk around with goatskin bottles supended from their necks. He had bet someone that he could carry a calfskin bag full of water, tied to him by an iron chain. Indeed, for seven consecutive days, from morning until evening, he carried the bag which hung from a chain on his bare shoulder, and he won his bet. He had the honor of a magnificent triumph and was accompanied by various musicians and all the water-carriers of Cairo, who must have been three thousand in number."

# 7
## Holidays and Amusements

WHEN THE ROLL OF A DRUM announced glad tidings from the Citadel, the city would be decked out with banners and cloth for seven days. The population was permitted to engage in unchecked, frenzied revelry.

The inhabitants, on these occasions, put on a display of unusual splendor. Banners, cloaks, scarves, precious silk cloth of white and other colors, velvet and muslin curtains were seen hanging from all the windows. Some people displayed armor, bows, cuirasses, helmets or coats of mail, and even jewels. This recalls a passage from Froissart's *Chroniques*: "And it should be known that all the large rue Saint Denis was so richly behung with camlet and silk cloth that you would have thought that the cloth cost nothing or that you were in Alexandria or Damascus." We should take into account this statement by Ibn Baṭṭūṭah: "In this city I was present at a celebration held because of the sultan's recovery from an illness. All the merchants decorated their markets; in front of their shops they hung jewels, striped cloth, and pieces of silk. They continued this celebration for several days." They even put up drapes inside their shops and scattered silk hangings on the ground in the streets. Here and there were set up basins full of syrup which was offered to the passers-by. On platforms, along the procession route, were singers, drummers, and flutists. From the attic windows were heard the women's happy trills, made, we are told by Pierre Belon, "by opening their mouths as wide as they can, emitting a falsetto sound, moving their tongues between their teeth and pulling them back toward the palate, and making a shrill sound like that at the end of the cry of the village women who sell milk in Paris."

On certain occasions such as victories or marriages of important courtiers or princesses, the markets took on a festive air, and the shops were decorated with hangings and were lighted at night. The entire city seemed to be ablaze because of the incalculable number of lights which burned everywhere; there were immense glass chandeliers, lanterns by the thousand, low-burning lamps, and fireworks. It is probable that the major role fell to the richest corporations, and, already under the Fatimids, the jewelers, the bankers, the goldsmiths, and the cloth merchants were mentioned as being responsible for setting up the hangings on the triumphal route.

Let us look at one of these processions. At the head came a company of soldiers. They were followed by a group of musicians, some blowing into long copper trumpets whose blasts contrasted with the frail and melancholy sound of the reed flutes played by another group. At some distance followed the singers, who chanted their poetry while beating gently on light drums.

The order of march of the officers who preceded the sovereign was strictly controlled by protocol. The spectators saw them come by in this order: ten foot-soldiers holding bared axes, then, mounted on white horses, two pages wearing yellow bonnets and yellow silk robes embroidered with gold. They brandished gold-brocaded banderoles, which were tied behind them to the ends of a sumptuous leather saddle cover so encrusted with gold that it seemed to have been made by a goldsmith. These were among the symbols of the monarchy and were, therefore, borne by two of the most important people of the state. Then appeared the sultan riding a completely caparisoned horse whose steel chamfron shone in the sun and whose neck was covered with a piece of yellow silk brocaded with gold. The royal costume was a dark splash in the midst of all this vivid color. The sultan's head was wrapped in a black silk turban whose end hung on his shoulders like the streamers of a flag. He wore a long black silk cloak with wide sleeves; the material was all of one color with no embroidery. He carried a battle saber held by a belt which went over his right shoulder and hung on his left side. One of the most important officials of the court held above the sultan's head a second symbol of sovereignty, a yellow gold–embroidered parasol with a little gilt ball on top of it and a gilt bird perched on the ball. A big, well-built fellow with fine military bearing walked at the sultan's right, carrying an enormous club with a gilt end. Ahead of the troops were borne several flags made of silk through which ran occasional gold threads. On top of the flagstaffs there were tufts of fur.

On April 30, 1500, the sultan went off to preside over the ceremony held at the breaking of the fast. He rode a white horse with an all-white silver saddle, and he was dressed in a white silk coat and white shoes with spurs incrusted with white silver; even the soles of his shoes were of white leather, and his skullcap was of white wool. This costume was rather strange. His dressing completely in white was taken as a bad omen, and the fact is that the sultan was deposed shortly afterward.

The procession sometimes included important prisoners. Some were on foot, others were astride mules, and all were chained. Soldiers followed carrying trophies taken from the enemy, especially their drums which were broken and their standards which were carried point down to symbolize defeat.

There was an exceptional day of celebration when a Dhoulqadirid prince was paraded by after he had been taken prisoner in a fierce battle. This took place in August, 1472, in the midst of the dog days. The sultan had the Bāb al-Naṣr and the Bāb Zuweila gates whitened and decorated with coats of arms. The capital was bedecked with magnificent hangings and the city was in a state of excitement, since everyone wanted to see the procession go by. Along the route a house rented at four ashrafis, and a place in a shop cost one ashrafi. The defeated prince on horseback wore a black robe and a voluminous turban; around his neck was an iron collar to which was attached a heavy chain, held by an officer riding at his side. This impressive procession consisted of officers who had taken part in the campaign, followed by their battalions. All the inhabitants of Cairo had crowded in front of the shops in order to see this spectacle. Singers were stationed from Bāb al-Naṣr to the foot of the Citadel. Batteries of kettledrums were heard at the Citadel; drummers and fife players were strung out in front of the shops. The prisoner was presented to the sultan inside the Citadel. Then he was stripped of his robe, dressed in a white one, and placed on a camel. Around his neck he wore an iron collar to which was attached a long iron rod with a bell at the end of it. Those of his relatives who shared his fate were placed bareheaded and completely nude on camels. In this manner the prisoners went down from the Citadel; they were preceded by heralds who shouted, "This is the punishment of anyone who plots against the sultan!" They arrived at Bāb Zuweila, and the prince was hanged on a hook in the middle of the gate. His body remained there a day and a night, then was removed, wrapped in a shroud, and buried north of the city. The flags and decorations were then taken down.

There was also the procession of the magistrates who used to go out to ascertain the time of the new moon at Ramaḍān. This procession was surrounded by innumerable round lanterns, wreaths of light, torches, and candles. Chandeliers, candelabra, and candles were also lighted in front of the shops, and perfume burners gave off a sweet scent.

One of the most popular spectacles was the procession of the mahmal, a "richly decorated, superb palanquin which was placed atop a sturdy camel, and served as a symbol of the desire for power. Its proud silhouette stood out above the Egyptian caravan as it crossed Arabia; the masters of Hejaz had to bow before it, and other caravans had to give way to let it pass."

"A large crowd of spectators always gathers the day that the mahmal is brought out. Here is how the day is celebrated. Four important cadis, the treasury minister, and the provost of the markets, all on horseback, are accompanied by the most learned jurists, the syndics of the corporations, and the greatest men of the empire. They all go together to the gate of the Citadel. The mahmal is brought out upon their arrival; it is carried on a camel and is preceded by the emir who is designated to make the trip to Hejaz that year. The emir is accompanied by his men and by water-carriers mounted on camels. All classes of the population, men as well as women, gather for this purpose; then they accompany the mahmal through the two cities of Cairo and Fostat. The camel drivers precede them, shouting at their camels to make them move on."

The procession soon degenerated into a bacchanalian orgy.

The soldiers, dressed in frightening burlesque costumes, demanded money of the laughing crowd. The devils of the mahmal, as they were called, committed such excesses that the government decided to forbid these manifestations. After many years, toward the end of the fifteenth century, the mahmal was preceded by a cavalcade of lancers dressed in scarlet who simulated battle as they rode by.

The people were sometimes invited to participate in wedding or circumcision ceremonies at which there was an extraordinarily magnificent display of torches, perfumes, and aromatics; the banquets at these celebrations were particularly copious. In March, 1501, a princess rode to the Citadel in a palanquin of gold brocade preceded by officers of the guard, chamberlains, noble guards in ceremonial dress, the governor of the city, the head of the army, the superintendent of the royal harem, the most important government officials, and the chief eunuchs. Two hundred ladies, the wives of the officers and officials, were part of the company. At the head of the procession was carried the trousseau offered by the sultan. Included were linens, a basin and a pitcher of rock crystal, and a gold brocaded tent.

Some funeral processions were rather picturesque, with their professional women mourners and their drummers.

In addition to the parades of triumph, there were also processions of disgrace. Bandits who had violated the common law were placed on camels and paraded through Cairo. A considerable crowd always gathered along the route, and the women hooted as the prisoners came by. Some criminals were whipped in public, placed on donkeys, and paraded naked and bareheaded through the city.

Bedouins who were punished for their misdeeds were treated in frightful fashion. The men had their necks in iron collars; the women and children were bound with ropes; sometimes women were made to wear around their necks the heads of men who had been killed during a punitive expedition. Sometimes the population was invited to witness a procession bearing an effigy made of the skin of an executed man stuffed with straw, dressed in a silk cloak, with a skull-cap placed on his head.

A heretic convicted of a crime against religion was placed on a camel, paraded through the city, and then hanged near the al-Malik al-Ṣālih Ayyūb school in the al-Qaṣreyn section.

Women of easy virtue who became the subject of a great deal of talk had their faces smeared with soot and were paraded through the streets on donkeys.

The joy shown by the people at some of the punishment which was meted out is an indication of the heavy tyranny which oppressed them. Writers have left us an account of the following horrible scene. The head of an important government official was carried about at the end of a pike and paraded through the streets of Cairo to the delerious cries of joy of the people, who were probably tired of having had to scrape and bow to the former minister. A half-dirhem was paid for the right to strike his face with a sandal, and twice that to cover it with filth. Frescobaldi saw the torture of a "criminal, entirely naked, placed on a camel, tied to pieces of wood in the form of a cross, with his arms bound so high that he seemed to be hanging. The executioner arrived, armed with a large bared saber, pricked the victim a little, then immediately struck him so great a blow with the saber above his navel that his body was cut in two. The arms and the upper part of the body remained suspended. The thighs and the rest of the trunk stayed on the camel. Only the intestines fell to the ground." A highway robber was paraded through the city, tied to a type of oddly shaped marionette, placed on a wheeled chariot, and turned by a mechanism. This sight upset the people considerably, but yet they crowded around to see it. A man caught digging in the tombs to steal shrouds was walked through the streets with his face flayed down to his neck and with the skin hanging on his chest; the bared bones of his skull could be seen.

\*     \*     \*

It does not appear that any space was set aside for collective festivities. Islam borrowed public baths from earlier civilizations, but nowhere in a Moslem city does one find places set up for popular performances, the theater, or circuses.

But curious gaping in the streets knows no place or time. We have had descriptions from countries other than Egypt of crowds gathering around a trainer and his bear or a tamer of monkeys who dance to the beat of a drum. These crowds get excited over a false holy man or hypocritical miracle-worker, or, as we have just seen, they crowd around a wretched person who is being beaten or led to the gallows. Arab writers of old also mention people who can swallow swords, sand, pebbles, soap, and ground glass or who can make things disappear or destroy them and then bring them back whole before the eyes of the gapers. Ibn Khaldūn says, without wanting to compromise himself too much, that he has heard that in Cairo there were specialists who taught birds to speak, who trained donkeys to do tricks, who could do sleight-of-hand stunts that fooled the spectators, and who taught people to sing, dance, and walk on tightropes high in the air.

There were certainly some places that were more suitable than others for public celebrations attended by all elements of the population. We are told that the dregs of the population, the debauched, the prostitutes went for their entertainment to the Bāb al-Lūq, the gathering place of magicians; thimble riggers; men who trained camels, donkeys, dogs, and monkeys to dance; traveling wrestlers; fortunetellers sitting behind their box of sand; and shadow-theater actors "who operated marionettes behind a cloth." Here were found, too, fencing masters who could handle all kinds of arms, especially the staff, and musicians who accompanied singers of songs of lament.

The animal trainers were the competitors of the snake charmers and the tightrope walkers. Pierre Belon wrote: "Among the Arabs in Cairo are many monkey trainers and drummers; during their act they beat a drum with their fingers while singing to the sound of this drum to which are attached several jingling pieces of copper; they hold it with their left hand and beat it with the right. They have a great gift for teaching monkey tricks to several kinds of animals. They teach them to goats, among others; they saddle them and place monkeys astride their backs and teach the goats to jump and buck like horses. They also teach donkeys to play dead, to wallow on the ground, and to pretend to kick out at the monkeys who climb on them. They also have trained female monkeys, which are very rarely seen since they are so undependable. They also have dog-faced baboons that are so gentle and well-trained that they go from person to person, among those watching the drummer play, hold out their hand indicating that money is to be put into it, and carry the money given them to their master."

Snake charmers walked about with sacks full of serpents which they could make do all sorts of fabulous tricks. With their breath they could make them fall as though they were dead; then, again with their breath, they could revive them and make them do things which seemed diabolic. One person saw a man take a cerastes with his bare hand from the bottom of a large jar containing several of these snakes. He put it on his bare head and covered it with his bonnet; then he removed it, placed it against his breast, and put it around his neck without having the snake do him any harm whatsoever. After that the same cerastes was approached by a chicken which it bit and which died several minutes later. Then to finish his show, the man took the cerastes by the neck and, beginning with its tail, ate the entire snake as easily and with as little repugnance as someone eating a carrot or a stalk of celery.

The tightrope walkers attracted crowds. One was seen above a pond in Cairo as he climbed up the ropes and walked on them backwards with his hands tied and his eyes blindfolded. Another tied a rope between the highest barracks of the Citadel and a minaret which was a good distance away. He walked on the rope, using his hands and his feet. Sometimes he threw burning pitch, and at other times he shot arrows from a powerful bow which he had with him. When the man had gone about half the distance he was to cover, he let himself fall suddenly. All the spectators cried out with fright and thought that the was going to be smashed to bits. But this was just a skillful trick; in his hand he held the end of a cord which had been carefully tied to the rope.

Arab writers show a certain amount of indignation when they speak about the horrible actions committed in public on the first day of the Coptic year. A New Year's Day "emir" was selected. He and his followers mounted on large camels and rode past the homes of the most important people of the city. He sent out requisitions and summoned those whom he claimed to be within his jurisdiction to appear before him.

He did all this in fun and was quite satisfied with even nominal offerings. Then singers and trollops carrying musical instruments, shouting, and openly drinking wine and beer appeared before this emir. In the streets people splashed each other with water which was dirty or was mixed with wine. Anyone who ventured out that day risked having his clothes ruined unless he paid a forfeit. At one time of the year, which cannot be exactly determined, the people threw hard-boiled eggs at each other and struck passers-by with leather straps. Toward the end of the fourteenth century the government tried to limit these manifestations to certain prescribed areas. But this type of amusement continued along the canals, the ponds, the Nile, and certain promenades. Everyone agreed that on New Year's Day pleasure and revelry went unbridled. Things went beyond the limits of decency and decorum, and excesses of debauchery and licentiousness were rampant. The day rarely went by without several murders.

The Nile festivals were occasions for the greatest rejoicing among the Egyptians. When it was announced that the river had reached its highest point, the inhabitants of Cairo, according to Maqrīzi, gathered to set up tents on the banks and the islands. Singers, those who ran games, owners of places of entertainment, courtesans, revelers, rowdy youths—all without exception went off to celebrate. Enormous sums were spent, and all forms of vice and corruption were in shameless evidence.

European travelers corroborated this observation of a rather despairing Arab chronicler. Trevisano wrote: "The dike was cut. It is customary, when the rising river has reached a certain point, for the sultan to send two important officials with their retinue to the limits of the city to cut the dike and let the water spread out on the land. A great throng of people turns out for this occasion, which is the most beautiful festival of the year. All the shops are closed, and all show great joy as they watch the water rush into the canal."

Several years later Leo Africanus was just as enthusiastic when he said: "During the first days of the flooding of the country, there is a great celebration in Cairo. There is so great a din of cries and music that the city seems turned upside down. Each family gets a boat which it decorates with the finest cloth and the most beautiful rugs and provides itself with a quantity of food, delicacies, and wax torches. The entire population is in boats and amuses itself as best it can. The sultan himself, with his principal lords and officials, takes part in the celebration. He goes to a canal called the Grand Canal, which is enclosed by a wall. There he takes an axe and breaks into the wall; the important persons of his entourage do the same so that the part of the wall which retains the water is demolished. The Nile immediately rushes into the canal with great violence, and then flows into the other canals of the suburbs and the walled city. As a result, on that day Cairo resembles the city of Venice; it is possible to reach by boat all the inhabited regions and all the localities of Egypt. The celebration lasts seven days and seven nights so that what a merchant or an artisan earns all year he spends that week on food, delicacies, torches, perfume, and musicians."

The island of Roḍah, facing Old Cairo, was also a center of amusement and a place to take walks. Here there were many parks where the inhabitants of Cairo and Old Cairo caroused, feasted, and enjoyed themselves. There were also many night festivals on the banks of the Raṭli Pond. The place was brilliantly lighted, and the people would rush off, crowding on the road, to see this spectacle. There were shadow-theater performances, vocal concerts, and other entertainment of that kind. These were pleasure-filled, festive nights that attracted an immense, joyful crowd.

It was in 1476 that one of the most pleasant sections of Cairo was finally founded, a place often admired by travelers of later periods. Earlier it had been a desolate, saline plain with occasional mounds, where tamarisks and acacias grew; little by little the site became empty, abandoned, and neglected. It was then that an important official of the Mamlūk Empire, named Azbak, decided to set up a stable for his camels there. When it was finished, he had the whimsical idea of having a house constructed on the site. He built several rooms, an apartment where he could entertain, and a pavilion. He brought some oxen and plows to remove the mounds of earth; then he had a lake dug and surrounded it by a walk. The wealthy people of Cairo followed his example and began to build splendid homes there. Everyone wanted to live in this neighborhood, which was named after its founder and to this day is called Azbakiyyah.

When the Nile reached its high mark, the dike was solemnly opened and the water flowed into Azbakiyyah Lake. This was the occasion for a great celebration. General officers were present, and crowds of people came to see the spectacle. In addition to the official banquet there were fireworks. Many boats were sailed on the lake. An Arab chronicler tells us that there were great festivities at which large amounts of money were madly spent amid wild carousing.

A more recent traveler tells us: "It was a plain situated in a conch shaped hollow completely surrounded by luxurious homes, and, while these homes embellished the site, the site itself offered a charming and varied view. There is no more beautiful sight than this terrain which is a vast basin filled with water eight months of the year and a cheerful, perpetual garden the other four months. In September one can go boating there; in April the area is verdant and covered with flowers. When the site is flooded, the water is furrowed by brigantines and gilt boats in which persons of quality sail at nightfall. On the shores of the lake there are numerous spectators who come to seek welcome relief from the heat of the day. When the water recedes, the earth is adorned with its usual beauty; there are as many palm trees and tamarisks as there are different types of grasses and fruits, which are the most pleasant sight imaginable. These are really enchanted gardens which spring up in the very place where boats sailed several months earlier."

The festivals on the Nile or on the Azbakiyyah Lake offered not only fireworks but magnificent lights which the Arab writers described. This tradition continued, for the art of illumination was carried to the highest degree of perfection. Towers, palaces, and even battles were formed with these lights. A European traveler wrote: "The front of each house had on it a particular figure; some represented the bodies of animals, others squares of arabesques arranged in somewhat the same fashion as those seen on their carpets. The wind cannot extinguish these lamps, and they remain lighted all night. One could see on the river two large ships which supported two very high, wooden pyramids completely covered with lamps placed very close to each other. Since the Nile was very high, they came up to the level of the banks of the river and could be seen, from any number of places, right down to their bases. The lamps of these pyramids changed constantly. Some of them descended as others replaced them very quickly; at other times they moved from side to side. These changes executed with such exactitude produced an admirable optical effect. No one on the outside could tell that they were attached to little pulleys or that there were men inside the structure who moved them. Not far from the pyramids was a third boat that carried a château made of fireworks and filled with rockets and petards; the effect was rather pleasant."

Leo Africanus informs us that the entire population of Cairo used to gather on the Azbakiyyah square each Friday after prayers and the sermon, because in this suburb were found some rather shady distractions such as those offered by taverns and ladies of ill repute. On this square, too, there were many entertainers, especially those who showed dancing camels, donkeys, and dogs. There were also men who fenced with sabers and staffs, and others who sang of the battles between the Arabs and the Egyptians during the conquest of Egypt. The mad, prankish, and vulgar acts that were committed there were both amusing and frequent.

# 8

## Urban Institutions

WE HAVE ALREADY ENCOUNTERED some religious monuments, and we shall see others, but now we want especially to consider those institutions which are useful to urban life in general. Since our recall of the past is incomplete, we realize how precarious our studies must be concerning the ancient period of Islamic Egypt. The old edifices have left us bas-reliefs which reveal all the aspects of current life; yet we are reduced to gathering meager information here and there in our reading, and to interpreting it to the best of our knowledge. But perhaps we insist too much upon details and incorrectly generalize exceptional facts. Voltaire said before we did: "An exceptional case is often taken for a general one." Of private life and the atmosphere in the market places we have only the accounts or even the troubled reflections of austere writers who severely censured the practices which stirred them to indignation and revolted them. All this amounts to very little, indeed.

A fifteenth-century author wrote: "The towns of Old Cairo and Cairo have so many public buildings that it is impossible to count or enumerate them. There are cathedral mosques, ordinary mosques, inns, schools, chapels, splendid residences, magnificent homes, sumptuous pavilions, tall palaces, delightful gardens, luxurious baths, covered markets with all sorts of merchandise, market-places full of anything one could desire, caravansaries crowded with transients and residents, and mausoleums that look like palaces."

The city was organized for commerce in that special buildings were set aside to store merchandise and others to lodge merchants. Depending upon the period or perhaps the destination of the building, these caravansaries were called by the Persian name "khan," by the Greek names "qaysaria" or "fonduk," or by the Arab name "wakala," from which the word "okelle" was derived in the Middle Ages. In the twelfth century, under the Fatimids, an official *"dar al-wakala"* was built to house merchants, especially Syrians and Mesopotamians, who came to Egypt on business trips.

A traveler wrote at the end of the fifteenth century: "There are in Cairo large fonduks, including a street along which there are rows of shops with three or four doors that are closed and guarded every night. All sorts of merchandise is found in these fonduks. Merchants and artisans, seated near their shops, display samples of all their articles. If you want to buy something of some importance or value, they take you into their shops and show you the marvelous things they have. As unbelievable as it may seem, each fonduk has more than a thousand of these stores. There is nothing in the world, including the most insignificant things, that cannot be found in the fonduks of Cairo."

Certain of these establishments have remained famous; through *A Thousand and One Nights* we are familiar with the Khan Masrūr, where slaves were sold.

These buildings were constructed in a uniform manner. The square structures were erected around a large paved court and had a portico which supported a gallery. The ground floor was made up of spacious stores; on the floor above were apartments or, more specifically, little unfurnished monks' cells with bare walls. The inhabitants had to furnish these themselves and prepare their meals in them.

There was only one door, similar to that of a citadel. This arrangement protected the inhabitants from being molested during uprisings. Everything was done to encourage business and protect merchandise; this was a sure means to economic prosperity. There was a distinct difference between the caravansaries or the covered markets and the *sūqs*. Merchandise was displayed in a single row and sold in the *sūqs*. In the vaster caravansaries, where there were several covered galleries, artisans could be seen at work in their shops.

At the entrance to the city, north of Bāb al-Futūḥ, there was a special khan where travelers were housed free of charge. Because of its location on the periphery of the city, it was soon used as a hospital for patients with contagious diseases. There was another khan which served as a sort of bank where merchants left their caskets of gold and silver. This establishment came to a rather sad end: the government seized the deposits when Egypt had to mobilize its forces against Tamerlane's invasion. The Qausūn khan, in the same neighborhood, was used by Syrian merchants to store their oil, sesame, soap, syrups, pistachios, walnuts, almonds, and carobs. In the Apple House, near the Mu'ayyad mosque, was found a large selection of fruit. Another khan, whose revenue was used to ransom prisoners of war, contained twelve shops, five booths, fifty-eight stores, six large rooms, a court, five attics, seventy-five rooms for lodgers, and five booths on the upper floors. Things became highly specialized; one building was used for products coming from Syria by sea and another one for merchandise coming from the same place by land.

Most of the indoor markets mentioned by Maqrīzi—nineteen of the thirty-two which could be located—were found in a small isosceles triangle whose point reached south to the

Bāb Zuweila and whose base was a line to the north stretching from the sultan Ghūri's tomb to the al-Azhar mosque. These establishments dealt especially in all kinds of cloth: wool, linen, inexpensive material, costly silk, trousseaux and finery for women, and trimmings. The names of the amber and carthamin markets explain sufficiently well what their products were. Some of the others housed artisans who made shoes, arrows, or chests. Five other indoor markets were grouped in the vicinity of the Qalāwun mausoleum, and seven of them were near the al-Ḥakim mosque.

We have some idea of the names of the markets in the middle of the fifteenth century, for Maqrīzi lists in Cairo thirty-seven *qaysarias*, nineteen fonduks, eleven khans, and three *dar al-wakalas*.

The Moslem city increased the number of bathhouses, the hammams, borrowed from antiquity without any change in their plan of construction: a dressing and rest room, a steam room, sometimes a room of intermediate temperature. The hammam played a hygienic role and a religious one in all the Moslem countries. According to the opinion of a Baghdad doctor, who wrote during the twelfth century, Egypt had its share of these bathhouses:

"The baths of Egyptians are admirable. I have seen none anywhere that are better constructed, better arranged, or more excellent in both beauty and realization. Their vats have a capacity of from two to four or more goatskin bottles. Water comes in through two taps, one for hot water and the other for cold water. First the water comes through these two taps into a very small, high vat; after the water from the taps mixes in the little vat, it then flows into the big one. About one-quarter of the large vat is above ground level; the other three-quarters is in the ground. Anyone wanting to bathe gets down into the vat and remains immersed in the water. Inside the baths there are cabins with doors, and in the area where one undresses there are also private cabins for persons of distinction so that they do not have to mix with the common people and do not appear naked before the public. This dressing room and its cabins are nicely arranged and well constructed. In the center there is a marble basin decorated with columns that support a dome. The ceilings of all these places are decorated with paintings; the walls are whitened and divided by panels; the floors are paved with squares of various colors; the marble of the inside rooms is always better than that of the outside ones. These baths are well lighted, and the vaults are very high. All the vases that are used are of varied, brilliant colors. In short, once inside, one does not want to leave again. Indeed, if a prince were to go to great expense to build a house and were to spare nothing in decorating it, he could not create anything more beautiful than these baths."

Breydenbach wrote at the end of the fifteenth century: "Some of our people went to the baths. There are in these countries very elegant, rich pools decorated with mosaics and various kinds of marble. The Saracens greatly enjoy this exercise and are marvelously skillful in rendering the bathers' limbs supple."

Hospitals were built in Egypt before the arrival of the Arabs; we are told that establishments of this type existed in Fostat from earliest times. We have not spoken of them at any length because of a lack of details. Public medical service had its beginnings under the reign of Ibn Ṭūlūn. The crowd in his mosque during Friday services was so great that a doctor had to be present to help those among the faithful who needed to be treated. The money for the hospital that he founded came from the revenue of the market where black slaves were sold and from other similar sources. Soldiers could not be treated there. The patients who were admitted had to undress and turn over their clothes and their money to a hospital employee who gave them a receipt for them. They put on special clothes, rested in beds, and received the required foods and medications free of charge. The day when they were able to eat a loaf of bread and a chicken, they were authorized to leave the hospital; whereupon their clothes and their money were returned to them. The prince visited the hospital every Friday, inspected the supplies, checked on the physicians, and questioned the sick, the infirm, and the insane.

The Ikhshidid princes also founded a hospital. We know for sure with what care the Fatimids supervised the teaching of medicine, but we have no information about the hospitals of their time.

Saladin turned one of the Fatimid palaces into a hospital. Physicians, ophthalmologists, surgeons, and an administrative director were assigned to it. It should be remembered that the famous medical historian Ibn Abi Usaibi'ah practiced there. Ibn Jubayr states:

"The hospital which we visited in Cairo adds to the sultan's glory. He has dedicated a remarkably beautiful and vast palace to this worthy cause in order to merit his reward and compensation in the hereafter. He has appointed a learned man as director, has entrusted the cabinets containing remedies to him, and has ordered him to prepare various types of potions and to administer them to the sick. In the small rooms of the palace, beds completely furnished with blankets are placed at the disposition of the patients. The director has servants under his command whose duty it is to check on the health of the patients morning and night and to give them suitable food and drink. Next to this establishment, but separated from it, there is another one for ailing women; they, too, have people to care for them. Adjoining these two buildings, there is another very large one, with iron bars on its windows, where the insane are housed. There are people who also check on their state of health every day and supply them with whatever is good for them."

The Qalāwun hospital was more important than all the other similar establishments in Cairo. It was an imposing structure built in a luxurious fashion which we can well imagine with our knowledge of the sovereign's mausoleum. It is estimated from the number of people who entered and left the building that four thousand patients a day were treated in the clinic during the fourteenth century. Every patient leaving the hospital received a gift of money and clothing. We are told that the food was very carefully prepared. A Moroccan traveler of the period does not hesitate to say that the furnishings rivaled in luxury and perfection those of the palaces of princes. All the personnel were well trained in their jobs, and all of them, without exception, from the doctors to the lesser employees, did their work with a sense of responsibility. The act setting up this wakf contains these admirable thoughts:

"I declare that the best opportunity to seize and the best act of philanthropy to perform are those which procure the well-being of others. One must assure the happiness of the poor man who is ill by offering him housing and medical care, which are expensive. Priority will be granted the most needy among the sick, the unfortunate, the weak, the helpless, and the wretched."

This hospital was established to treat ailing Moslems, men

or women, residents or transients from all countries and provinces, without distinction as to origin or rank, regardless of the illness of which they complained, whether slight or serious, obvious or subtle, physical or mental. Poor patients, male or female, remained under treatment in the hospital until they were cured. There were also provisions made for the distribution of medicines and potions to outpatients. The patients were separated according to precise categories; there were rooms reserved for infectious diseases, ophthalmology, surgery, and enteritis. One reads of even rather unexpected provisions in the wakf regulations, such as the one authorizing purchase of palm-frond fans to keep the patients comfortable during the hot season.

The ribat was at first a unit of frontier guards composed of warrior monks. In the fourteenth century this institution sheltered individuals who had neither resources nor family. We know even of a house of retreat for rejected women who wanted to meditate away from the everyday world before remarrying. Under the influence of mysticism, the ribat became a Sufi monastery, although the usual name for this type of monastery was *khanaqah*. The most famous one in Egypt offered asylum to members of a contemplative order.

The words "monastery" and "monk" have certain precise meanings in Christianity. It is, therefore, important to avoid any possible misunderstanding. The Moslem monastic regime cannot be compared with the severe reclusion of Christian monasteries. Unlike Christianity, Islam has never considered the body a tattered garment and has never scorned life on earth. Moslem monasticism corresponds more closely to the third orders of Christianity in that the members of the order do not completely renounce the material world. As in the third orders, membership is open to everyone. This should be quite obvious, since there is no clergy in Islam. The rules vary according to the charter of the wakf. Certain monasteries admitted married monks, who, of course, did not live in the monastery.

Before pointing out several excesses which were practiced, we should consider the page written by Ibn Baṭṭūṭah on the monasteries of Cairo: "The emirs of Cairo try to surpass each other in the construction of buildings. Each monastery is dedicated to a congregation of monks, most of whom are of Persian origin. These are people who are instructed and well versed in Sufistic doctrine. Each monastery has a superior and a guardian. The order reigning within is marvelous. Here is one of the customs regarding meals: the monastery servant goes to the monks in the morning, and each one tells him what he wants to eat. When they gather for their meals, each one has placed in front of him his bread and his soup in a separate bowl, which he shares with no one. They have two meals a day. They are served sugar delicacies on the night which falls between Thursday and Friday. They are given soap with which to wash their clothes, oil to fill their lamps, and enough money to pay the entrance price to the baths. This is how the unmarried monks live. The married ones have separate monasteries. Among the obligations imposed upon them are those which require their presence at the five canonical prayers, the duty to spend the night in the monastery, and to gather in the chapel inside the monastery. Another of their customs is for each one of them to be seated on a prayer rug which is his private property. During their morning prayers, each monk is responsible for reading a part of the Koran, so that among them all the entire book is read."

Under the reign of the Mamlūks, the brotherhoods became

a political force with which the government had to reckon.
The priors were, therefore, appointed by the sultan, so that
he could maintain some control. Those whom we can call
the secular clergy, for the sake of clarity, such as the madrasah teachers, the cadis, and the muftis, were jealous of
these monks, who were often foreigners. We know the
monks through the criticism of these people; we should,
therefore, accept their judgments rather cautiously. They
frowned upon these monks who claimed that they had only
to listen to their hearts, after indulging in song and dance
sessions, to attain God's love. But they especially feared that
the monks would gain influence over the popular classes,
those whom it was particularly important to keep in check.
Certain incidents arose. In 1496 the Sufis in one monastery
revolted against their superior, a well-known writer. They
tore off their robes, threw them into the basin set aside for
ablutions, and were on the point of attacking the superior.
The historian who informs us about this incident says: "Dis-
orders followed that would take too long to recount."

Egypt, we know, had no monopoly on monks who sometimes abandoned their religious mission to stir up the masses.
Conflict with civil authorities stemmed from this. We are
familiar with Cardinal Pierre Damien's severe remarks about
certain Italian monks, "city hermits, public square recluses,
universal monks, people who, under the guise of monastic
profession, try to take command of the people." It was, indeed, under the Mamlūks that the congregations, whose influence was growing, began to develop in a dangerous direction. Of course, it is hardly fair to make generalizations from
the few remarks which we must consider. It is, however,
striking to see how often the most religious writers lashed
out sarcastically at these men, scandalously attired in rags

or cheap finery, who had decided to shake off the yoke of the rules of decency which were commonly obeyed throughout the world. Ibn Khaldūn struck out at the inhabitants of the monasteries—"people who make a display of their devotion to enhance their own worth, while insulting the majesty of God." They fasted and prayed only when they were strictly obliged to; they indulged in all the permitted pleasures and observed only those obligations whose omission would place them in error. They certainly did not go to the trouble of entering into the spirit of the laws.

The pious institutions, schools, mosques, and monasteries had a charitable character, for the gifts of these religious establishments made possible the distribution of food and clothing. But the most pious work of all was the gift of a public fountain. A French writer of the period tells us: "The greatness of a people should be judged by what it does to obtain water." This thought coincides with a declaration of Mohammed engraved on one of the fountains of Cairo. "When the Prophet was asked what was the worthiest of acts, he replied, 'The offer of drinking water.'" In the Near East water is of vital necessity; this is why there were fountains in most homes during the Middle Ages. Devout persons, thinking of those who were less fortunate, had public fountains set up. This good deed offered drinking water to the inhabitants of a city, but, perhaps even more importantly, it supplied them with water for ritual ablutions. The use of these fountains was, therefore, free to the public. They were supplied by water carriers. Suction brought the flow of water through brass pipes, and the passers-by drank from cups chained to the fountain. A traveler at the end of the fourteenth century remarked: "The great number of fountains seen in the city is a sign of nobleness." At first they were part of the other monuments, such as schools and monasteries. Later, under the Mamlūks, the fountains were very picturesque, independent structures with wide bays and bronze bars; above them there were loggias which served as primary schools.

In the fifteenth century very little open space was left in the city. As a result, the public buildings which were erected had to be smaller than the earlier ones. Schools were built on a reduced scale, and the central open courtyard was eliminated. The entire building was covered by a roof which contained an opening to admit daylight. Of course, housing for teachers and students in these buildings was out of the question. Thus, from the fifteenth century on, no difference can be seen between the schools and the mosques. There is a rectangular prayer room; the lateral *liwans* are reduced to mere recesses, and the only reminder of the old central court is a slight difference in floor level.

# 9
## The Magnificent Cemeteries

THE CEMETERIES, vast necropolises in the narrowest sense of the word, were located in the western suburbs of Cairo.

These were at first south of the Citadel. Ibn Jubayr mentioned this "plain that is called the terrain of the tombs of the martyrs, that is, of those who gave proof of their faith. It appears as though it is full of the mounds of tombs without any buildings; it is remarkable that in reality the Qarāfa Plain is entirely built up with inhabited oratories and tomb monuments which serve as refuges for foreigners, the learned, the devout, and the poor. Each building receives a monthly subsidy granted by the sultan. But going off to live in Qarāfa suits both the good man and the evil one; you can find whatever you are looking for there. The solitude it offers pleases ascetics; its protection from the law pleases brigands."

A miracle used to take place there which is mentioned for the first time at the beginning of the sixteenth century. Baumgarten wrote: "Outside the city, on the banks of the Nile, we were shown a mosque. We were told that when a religious service is held there the dead leave their tombs and stand motionless during the entire holy ceremony; then they disappear. Everyone in Cairo is aware of this fact." Several years later Agrippa d'Aubigné mentioned this miracle in his *Tragiques*.

The Moroccan, Ibn Baṭṭūṭah, also saw only the southern cemetery. He wrote: "The inhabitants of Cairo build elegant chapels which they surround with walls and which look like houses. Quite close by, they erect lodgings for men who read the Koran in beautiful voices day and night There are some who build chapels and schools near mausoleums They go to spend the night from Thursday to Friday there with their wives and their children and march in procession around the famous tombs."

During the same period European travelers pointed out this singular aspect of the cemeteries: "East of the city, about one mile away, stretches the immense and very famous Saracen cemetery. Rising above the tombs, there is such a great number of chapels and buildings that one would think he was looking at a vast city instead of a cemetery." Another one said: "There are large cemeteries where the tombs of the Moslems are found and where magnificent monuments have been erected of marble, porphyry, alabaster, and other fine stones, admirably constructed and gilded. I have not seen any of comparable magnificence in all of Christendom. These are tombs of old sultans, emirs, and noble Saracens."

With Piloti, in 1420, we discover the tombs of the southern region: "One mile away from Cairo is a city which is not walled, is as large as Venice, and has tall structures and short ones; in this city are buried all those who die in Cairo. Every Saracen and townsman has a building in this city. In the short ones, they bury their dead, and in the tall ones all the lords who own them give alms to the poor every Friday. It is on this day that they have their holiday, say their prayers, and prepare large meals of meat. And it is on this day that all the poor of Cairo go there to eat and to receive the money which is given them."

It is, indeed, in this city of tombs, where private citizens were buried at one time, in a desolate area, at the edge of the desert, east of the town, that splendid mausoleums began to be built to receive the remains of the Mamlūk rulers. It would seem that these princes, whose lives were so full of excitement, wanted to have their tombs in a deserted, lonely place, far from pleasant gardens, far from all greenery, far from the eyes of the living world, and far from the tumult of the Citadel, the seat of their power, as though to keep the noises of life from troubling their last sleep. The upward thrust of the domes and the minarets adds an atmosphere of both peace and gloom to the area. These startlingly white, shadowless monuments stand in an unchanging, implacable light which never permits the softening of a single angle. At twilight, these become silhouettes standing out against the sky.

The pilgrim Breydenbach came here on his way from the Citadel. He wrote: "We came down a steep slope, not without danger, and crossed several cemeteries; then we arrived at the tombs of the sultans. For each sultan has an individual mosque built in the spot he has chosen. The present sultan, whose name is Qāyit Bey, had a large, very spacious one built with an elegantly decorated, very high tower. He had large houses built all around it, with a great number of rooms like a monastery. Here he maintains priests of the law and of the cult of Mohammed."

Let us stop for a moment at Qāyit Bey's monumental tomb, which intrigues us with its playful spirit. Here we see the birth of a highly decorative art full of charm and grace. We become aware of the fine, shaded expressions of the arabesques which are of unequaled softness. This is the world of capricious reverie, but it is also the triumph of the flamboyant. Here elegance reaches its culmination, and the art of decoration attains its highest degree of magnificence. The artists worked with such easy talent that they appeared to be playing. The visitor seems to be welcomed and put at ease by the building. When trying to trace the delicate combinations of lines, which are almost a series of arpeggios, he forgets whether he is dealing with sculpture or with the work of a goldsmith. The alternating courses of light and dark marble and the festooned arch stones seem to smile down at us. A period when mausoleums take on a friendly, gentle air is, indeed, a curious one. These Tombs of the Caliphs, as they are called—just as famous as the Aliscamps were at one time—this funeral field, this immense plain punctuated by domes and minarets, have absolutely nothing sad about them.

# 10

# The Royal Palace
## and the Esplanade of the Citadel

LET US CLIMB TO THE TOP of the Muqaṭṭam, as we did at the beginning of this book, and read once again the passage written by Gobineau:

"At first one sees below a vast square and, on the opposite side, the mosque of Ḥasan; then, to the left and right, stretches the city, cut by thousands of streets, cluttered with mosques and large buildings, and embellished in a hundred places by clusters of trees and gardens. It is not gay, it is not strange, and it is not majestic in the usual sense of the word since there is a complete absence of symmetry; but it is big, vast, airy, full of life, warmth, freedom, and, therefore, of beauty. Doubtless, one can see other cities which better fulfill certain conditions leading to prefection. Nothing here is perfectly straight; but if regularity is lacking, the general aspect is serious and noble, although varied, and there is a feeling of power here. Even though this is not a creation of antiquity, it does date back to times which are already quite old, times in which there was no lack of faith and thought, courage and wealth, and even energy."

This is a perfect observation point for contemplating this majestic city. We find ourselves in an amphitheater of light, limited to the north and the south by the minarets of the royal tombs of the Mamlūk sultans. In the foreground, the mosque of the sultan Ḥasan stands out boldly; the vastness of this stone colossus is brought out even more sharply by the mass of buildings which stretch out far beyond it. Our eyes linger for a long time on the flat countryside outside the city, far from the river behind which the row of pyramids stands out on the horizon like a series of minute dots.

The Sultan Ḥasan Madrasah, probably Islam's most beautiful monument, will help us understand the general building plan of an edifice dedicated to the teaching of the four Sunnite rites. Seen from the inside, the school consists of a central court bordered by four *liwans*; the one facing Mecca is larger than the others. The interior structure, therefore, takes on the appearance of a cross. We have no reason to attribute this to Christian influence. On the outside, the building is square or rectangular, since between the branches of the cross there are apartments for the teachers and some of the students of the four rites.

The massiveness of a powerful-looking building with high, austere walls seems to menace the Citadel which stands across from it. How many rebellions, how many bloody battles have taken place under these walls! This is, as a matter of fact, a school dedicated to peaceful, pious instruction. Because of its location, however, it has played a political role. In every uprising in Cairo, the first objective of the rebels has been to turn this mosque into a stronghold. From the outside, it looks like a cube-shaped fortress whose height is accentuated by vertical grooves in which narrow windows are set and by a projecting cornice running along the top of the walls. The entrance to the building is a corridor with a double turn, which opens suddenly, with no warning, onto a large, airy courtyard surrounded on four sides by gigantic, cradle-vaulted vestibules. The general rhythm of the structure is certainly heavy, but this heaviness is lightened by the harmonious balance of its masses.

The site chosen for this structure was just opposite the fortified castle which dominates the city of Cairo, and the architect was inspired by the challenge that this offered. Erecting this austere monument in the shadow of the almost insolent hostility of the Citadel walls was indeed a challenge. Sultan Ḥasan took advantage of every inch of the Citadel to make it look as though it were stretching in preparation for a proud, yet calm, leap. The cyclopean mosque seems to be intent on crushing the Citadel. It is enhanced by its admirable location and is set off by an esplanade which separates it from its rival. The Olympian beauty of this fortress-mosque, which somewhat recalls the Cathedral of Albi, has qualities that appeal to universal reason. As admirable in its realization as it is in the absolute logic of its conception, it is an incisive, flawless work which makes all commentary superfluous. It is an architectural peak from which Mamlūk art, with its undeniable charm, could move in no direction but down. In Egypt it is the most nearly perfect, the most homogeneous monument, and the one most worthy of standing side by side with the amazing vestiges of Pharaonic civilization. The lamentable historical conditions under which it was built should make us appreciate it even more. It stands in contradiction to the usual belief that a stable and orderly state is an indispensable prerequisite for the long and exacting building of so bold and so splendid a stone monument. It took seven years of work and hardship, if we are to believe the statement of the sultan himself: "If I were not afraid that people would say that the sultan of Egypt is incapable of finishing a structure which he has begun, I would abandon the work because of the expense involved." In addition, there were political difficulties which led to the dethroning of the sultan. It is ironical that this ruler who, like the ancient

Pharaohs, had built himself a tomb which was to be eternal, was assassinated and was never placed in a sepulcher.

The plague of 1348, which wiped out two-thirds of the population of Florence, caused a horrible number of deaths in Cairo. It serves no purpose to mention that entire fortunes went to the public treasury because there were no surviving heirs. We are told that some estates passed through the hands of four or five successive heirs in a single day. This was during the first reign of the sultan Ḥasan; the unexpected influx of money may have been the reason for his lack of thrift.

Perhaps Saladin created a citadel with the intention of calming a restive people and resisting possible attack by an outside enemy. Marcel Clerget wrote: "Under his successors, the Citadel took on the definitive appearance of a fortified palace-city. The two enclosures became one, little by little; the legal and administrative buildings multiplied and invaded the area at the foot of the mountain spur; more gates were built into the walls. There were eventually a series of pavilions for the Court, a room where justice was meted out, magnificent stables, bathhouses, a mosque, and gardens which were abundantly supplied with water by a clever system of wells, conduits, and saqiahs. A larger and larger population gravitated around these services; there were markets and merchants who supplied staples, arms, and household utensils on the spot. Casanova correctly said that it was a sort of Potsdam or little Versailles with narrow, winding streets cut into the rock."

The large audience room of the Citadel had been redone by Mohammad ibn Qalāwun. He erected a splendid dome over it, enlarged it, furnished it with superb columns from Upper Egypt, refinished it with marble, and placed in the center the royal throne made of ivory and ebony. He made the room much higher and had a very wide and long square built in front of it. The door to the room had an artistically wrought iron grill to keep people from entering. For the sultan himself there was a door which was usually closed; when he wanted to hold an audience, the door was opened so that he could see, through it or through the grilled windows, the major part of his army on the square. He regularly presided at audiences on Mondays and Thursdays.

A travel account informs us: "Toward the center of this city of Cairo, on the east side, on a spur of the mountain, stands the sultan's castle, vast, beautiful, and very suitably built up and ornamented with military buildings, palaces, offices, and other imperial splendors. It is said that it is one mile around and its distance from the city is the range of one ballista. Ten thousand cavalrymen are stationed there, specially assigned to guard the sultan, without counting those who live in the above-mentioned city. The foundations of the Castle, as well as the whole edifice, are made of soft, white stone. This castle, in spite of the large military installation, has no springs of water, and its walls, we are given to understand, break easily."

Here is Khalil al-Zahiri's description in the middle of the fifteenth century: "The royal residence, where the throne of the Empire is located, is known today by the name of the Castle of the Mountain. This palace is unequaled in area, brilliance, magnificence, and height. It is surrounded by ramparts, moats, towers, and numerous iron gates which make it impregnable. It would take too long to give a detailed description of the palaces, rooms, salons, belvederes, galleries, courts, squares, stables, mosques, schools, markets, and baths which are found in the palace; we must limit ourselves to pointing out the most remarkable things and those which can best give an idea of the greatness of the Empire. The Multicolored Palace is composed of three main buildings used for official ceremonies. They are covered with marble of different colors, and the ceilings are painted in gold and blue and are decorated with various paintings. The Great Hall has nothing in the world to equal it; it stands alone and is separated from the Multicolored Palace; it is surmounted by a very high, beautiful, green dome. That is where the royal throne is kept. This dome, which is of the most beautiful architecture inside and out, rests on marble columns. The Great Mosque of the Citadel is equally wondrous; I am assured that it can hold five thousand faithful. Columns of tremendous size are seen within. It is flanked by two minarets of striking architecture. In this Castle are found little apartments for the sultan's private gatherings; they are of astonishing elegance and richness. A certain number of mansions house the sultan's wives. The Mamlūk barracks are twelve in number; each one of them is almost as long as a street and can hold up to a thousand Mamlūks. The interior court of the palace is of enormous size; in it are a vast garden and a little pond. The stables in which the monarch's horses are kept are also very vast and great in number."

Sixteenth-century travelers insisted that this castle was of very little military value. Jehan Thenaud wrote: "The sultan's palace is hardly less spacious than the city of Orleans. When we entered, two bombards were fired. There were fifty musicians with various instruments. We passed a court in which there were certainly five hundred Mamlūks in formation, with their long white robes and their round green and black hats. We passed another court at the entrance to which were several harnesses and machines used to break down walls; there were also armorers and polishers. Here there were about two thousand Mamlūks in even better form than the others. At the head of this court, on a high, richly carpeted stone, the sultan sat cross-legged, tailor fashion. In front of him the earth was covered with a rug easily twenty feet square. His robe was of yellow taffeta, and he wore on his head a very tall turban made of fine cloth from India and fashioned into six peaks, two of which were in front, two others on the right, and two more on the left. This long-peaked headdress had been in style for only about twenty years at that time."

The Venetian Trevisano, having been received by the ruler of Egypt, added: "Cairo has a citadel which is not very strong; its enclosure is about a three-mile area. It is built on high ground formed of rock, and it dominates the entire city. Within was the very beautiful and very pleasant residence of the sultan. There is no other fortified place in Cairo. This citadel would not be called a fortress back home; it would be called a magnificent palace."

During his solemn audiences, the sultan sat under a gold brocade canopy. The door to the arsenal was decorated with standards, streamers, and armor such as caparisons, coats of mail, axes, and sabers. The most detailed description of a reception at the Citadel is that of the Florentine Felice Brancacci, who obtained an audience with the sultan Barsbey in 1422:

"One hour before daybreak, our interpreters came for us and brought horses with them. One of the lords whose duty it was to receive ambassadors was with them, as were several other officials, some on foot, others on horseback. We set out for the sultan's castle which was about two miles away and situated on a height. We went as day was breaking, but we waited about an hour outside the first gates. The sun was already high, and Mamlūks, who are the nobles of high and low rank, kept going into the castle. There was a great crowd of them; they were dressed in their usual style of white linen which hung to the ground and were draped in large pieces of very fine linen with sleeves decorated with blue embroidery forming bands of designs peculiar to these people. Almost all of them wore this uniform. Toward the middle of the third hour, we went up to the castle by means of a stairway about eighty yards wide but which was steep and very inconvenient for the horses. We thus arrived at a gate through which we entered a large court, where we sat down among a great number of Mamlūks and waited for half an hour. Then, having gone through another gate, we went along several vaulted passageways, between two rows of Mamlūks facing each other, with lance in hand, until we came to another door guarded in the same way. Continuing through more vaulted corridors, we came out into a court where there were again men armed with lances and lined up in the same fashion. There we were very carefully searched down to our breeches to make sure we were not hiding arms. Finally we came to the sultan's residence after having climbed eight staircases on which there were always men armed with lances. The lances of these men had iron tips with several points and are similar to our halberds; they clashed them over our heads as we went by. Everywhere at these guard posts there were about twelve lancers. The room we entered—the one in which the sultan sat—was divided like a church into three naves separated by stone columns; the center nave was much larger than the side ones. These naves were open on the side through which we entered, but a net hung over the openings from top to bottom. They were paved with inlaid marble, and almost half their surface was covered with a rug. Facing the entrance, there rose a sort of platform with steps on both sides. Seated right on the floor of this platform was the sultan. The platform had no parapet in front, and the lateral steps had no ramps; he was perfectly visible from everywhere. He was dressed in linen like the others. He was about thirty-eight or forty years old and had a brown beard. Directly behind his shoulders stood a great number of Mamlūks. One of them held a sword and its scabbard in his hand, another carried a ewer, and a third one carried very high on his right shoulder a solid gold rod about a yard long and an inch thick. Near them, as well as on the side steps and at the foot of the platform, stood a great number of Mamlūks. This large assembly was arranged in such a way that it brought to mind triumphal scenes that are seen in paintings. Every place, especially on the steps at the foot of the columns, there were musicians playing viols, rebecs, lutes, muted instruments, and cymbals all at the same time, accompanying singers with a great deal of noise and occasional unison. I, whose eyes were dazzled and whose ears were deafened, and who had, moreover, to kiss the ground with each step, renounce trying to give an orderly description. In addition, two men grabbed each one of us by the shoulders and led us in this cramped manner as though we were pack animals. Each time they wanted us to kiss the ground, they cried out something in their language loudly enough to deafen us. They made us kiss the ground this way seven or eight times. When we had come to within about twenty-five yards of the sultan, we stopped and the noise ceased. We were told to be brief in this first interview, during which three shining axes were constantly brandished over our heads. We had hardly said to our interpreter a dozen words introducing our subject, when we were interrupted with, 'Enough! Enough!,' and, after having been made to kiss the ground, we were led backwards to the entrance of the room. There, having once more kissed the earth, we were able to turn our backs on the sultan and leave. And the sultan left the room."

This last description of the Citadel which we can repeat, that of Pierre Belon, not only offers similar details but renders final homage to the Mamlūk sultans: "The buildings of the Castle of Cairo, the beautiful rooms and salons, and the paintings that are found there give evidence of the magnificence of the Circassians, who ruled over Egypt not very long ago. The walls are covered with marble to the height of a man all around the doors and the windows; there is a border more than a foot wide inlaid in the Damascene manner with mother of pearl, ebony, crystal, marble, coral, and colored glass. The Castle sits upon very hard rock into which steps have been cut to make the ascent easier. The site of the Castle is, therefore, on high ground and is almost round; there are several big, round towers, made in the ancient way, which are not of very good material. The court of the Castle is big and spacious, and the building is very pleasant and agreeable, for as one looks out of the windows, here and there, where there is a good open view, one can see almost all of Egypt. The Castle of Cairo, compared with other fortresses, must not be considered very strong."

This was, indeed, the opinion of the government when, menaced by a rebellion in December, 1500, it decided to reorganize the defenses of the Citadel. Batteries of canon were placed on the ramparts, the walls and the towers were repaired, and above the Mudarradj staircase was built a gate which still exists; the Chain Gate was surrounded by a tower, built of cut stone, in which there were archers' win-

dows and little doors. The sultan blocked the openings to
the hippodrome, to the Court of the Arabs, and to the stables
near the entrance ramp. Then he ordered that the Sultan
Ḥasan Madrasah be demolished. A part of the façade was
attacked, but when, after three days' work, nothing much
had been accomplished, the project was abandoned. The
people were quite upset over the proposed demolition of so
splendid a monument, the like of which existed nowhere
else in the world and whose destruction would have served
no purpose. Besides, the undertaking proved to be impossible,
and it was more dignified to abandon it that to admit that it
could not be done. The sultan had fodder, biscuits, cheese,
and other essential staples brought to the Citadel. The cis-
terns were filled, and the kitchens were stocked with whatever was necessary to withstand a two months' siege. The
staircases of the Sultan Ḥasan Madrasah were destroyed.
War materials, especially pieces of wood for building ladders
and barricades, were brought to the Citadel. Swords, coats
of mail, corselets, cuirasses, bows, and arrows were taken
from the arsenal and distributed to the troops.

A little later the water problem was thought of. In about
April, 1507, the sultan had the Old Cairo aqueduct destroyed
and ordered that a new one be built. A well was dug at the
point of departure and communicated with the Nile by
means of a conduit; the water was raised to the desired level
by series of *sakiehs*. This aqueduct, which went as far as the
Citadel, was built on arches supported by pillars. The people
of the time considered this piece of work a great wonder, but
they were furious at the sum of money spent for its construction, money which was raised through unfair means
and confiscations. Seen from above, this aqueduct, which is

now rather dilapidated, looks, as it "lies on a desolate plain, like a snake's skeleton with dislocated vertebrae."

In the Citadel there were a certain number of prisons. A dungeon which was built at the end of the thirteenth century was used as a prison by the emirs. After it had been in use for forty years, the inspector of buildings went down into it to arrange for repairs. He was struck with horror by the total darkness, frightened by the number of bats, and sickened by the foul odor which impregnated this underground prison. He had it filled up immediately. But another one existed which was just as sadly notorious; it was called the *Arquana*, the Oozer, probably because of its dampness. It was used for political prisoners or for merchants who had broken the law. Some of the prisoners were put in irons and kept there for many years. Doubtless escape was possible, but not without great danger. We have only rather late descriptions of these prisons given us by European travelers.

"One sees jails and prisons among which there is still the prison where innocent Joseph was kept and where he interpreted the dreams of his companions who were incarcerated with him. At present, it is a foul, stinking place where the poor prisoners are mistreated, tied in irons to logs, and bound in chains; if they were not given alms, they would be condemned to die seated on the damp ground and on the filth which is piled up everywhere."

Among the outbuildings of the royal palace of the Citadel visited by some travelers were the sultan's stables, in which there were not only the ruler's private horses but also certain curious and beautiful animals. First of all, there were elephants. A traveler stated: "We saw three of them; each one was tied by his neck and his feet to posts and pickets, by means of very big iron chains. Although they are without a doubt monstrous animals and not very pleasant looking, they seem, nevertheless, because of their enormous size and their height, to possess that great strength of which the Holy Scriptures speak."

But it was probably the giraffe which created the most excitement.

"It is of such great height that a tall man could hardly reach with his fingertips that animal's croup. It is a very beautiful and graceful looking animal; it has a very curly coat, and its skin is quite similar to a deer's. Somehow or other, its entire body is covered with light marks. Its neck is very frail and long and is carried high when the animal walks. On its head it has two little horns and its forehead is pointed in the shape of a diamond. Its forelegs are much longer than the hind ones, and, because of this peculiarity, everyone agrees that the animal looks deformed. Its tail, which it hardly moves, is thin and has very little hair on the end."

It is possible that the sultan also kept wild animals. We are told that on April 30, 1515, large elephants, lions, and other wild animals fought in the hippodrome.

\*     \*     \*

If the idea of a "commune" had existed in the Moslem world, the Sultan Ḥasan building facing the seat of government would have represented the threat of the city against the state. In any event, the presence in this place of so formidable a bastion constituted a permanent danger. Moreover, this was not always a calm and peaceful spot, since it was here that the bloodiest adventures in the history of the Mamlūks took place; this area was the theater of the most extraordinary scenes of savagery. Those were times of dis-

tressing insecurity and upheaval when furious waves beat
up against the Citadel. This esplanade was, all things considered equal, comparable to the Piazza della Signoria in
Florence, in that it was here that the heart of political life
beat during the two centuries of domination by the Mamlūk sultans.

Between the two fortresses, the real one and the Sultan
Ḥasan mosque, were held royal feasts and banquets for ambassadors in times of peace. The area was really quite an
extensive one where people were able to take pleasant walks.
On this flat square there were always an infinite number of
people on horseback or on foot, as well as many soldiers and
employees of the sultan. Camels, donkeys, and horses were
sold here.

Toward the south was the hippodrome, the tournament
ground, where jousters displayed the skillful parrying which
so delighted the Mamlūks. Polo matches, then called "horseback tennis," were held in this sand arena. A traveler at that
time wrote: "The sultan sometimes amuses himself with
his officers and other noblemen of his army. The type of
amusement that they engage in is the same as that which
is practiced in Christian countries by shepherds who play
with a ball and bent sticks. There is this difference: the nobles
and their sultan never strike the ball unless they are on
horseback, and, in their own way, they have made a military
game of this, judging the horse and the rider's strength,
agility, and other martial qualities."

A ball was placed in the middle of the field, and two parallel lines were drawn, one at either end. The riders were
divided into two teams. Each player carried a mallet with a
long handle and tried to hit the ball across the opposing line.
We are told the following: "On the very edge of this field,

151

there is a vast, tall palace from which the sultan's wives and the other nobles can watch the players and especially the sultan himself, without mingling with the large crowd of spectators. Every time that the sultan takes his turn at striking the ball, everyone congratulates and applauds him, innumerable trumpets sound, and a great number of deep sounding drums boom out in the midst of shouts and calls."

In this hippodrome, too, the Mamlūks showed their skill as archers. This was the national sport of the Turkish Mamlūks. A pigeon was enclosed in a gold or silver cage resembling a gourd. The contestants fired their arrows as they rode by at full gallop, trying to shoot the pigeon.

Giacomino of Verona witnessed the daily military exercises of the Mamlūks: "Each morning the soldiers assemble in front of the Castle gate. They are all armed with bows and ride little horses the size of light chargers and palfreys; I have never seen a battle-steed among them. All the riders were poorly protected and had only little iron helmets on their heads. Only a few of them wore cuirasses; others had only leather armor. Not one has any protection for the arm carrying the bow, for his thighs, or his legs. They have short stirrups, and when they want to use their bows, they stand up in their stirrups and then shoot their arrows. I have seen all the sultan's horses wearing covers embroidered with gold and silk."

According to another fourteenth-century traveler: "The horsemen all ride in low saddles and short stirrups, like ladies. On the rear part of each of these saddles there is a ring in which is fixed in a very military manner a club, a type of cudgel, for the protection and the defense of the rider. All the riders, without exception, are armed with curved swords; in addition, many are excellent archers, especially the Turks whose bows are made of curved horn and whose arrows have a polygonal section, like lances; the head of these arrows is planted in the shaft like the blade of a knife in its handle."

At the end of the fifteenth century similar information was furnished: "Every day, or at least three times a week, the palace Mamlūks go to the plain at the foot of the mountain to engage in their warlike maneuvers. By scaling ravines and precipices, they carry out their military exercises and, thus, train their horses in the plains as well as the hills."

This place had its apotheosis during the reign of Sultan Ghūri at the beginning of the sixteenth century. The ruler had the ground level of the hippodrome raised four cubits; it was all smoothed off and covered with gravel. A pavilion and a room to be used as a tribunal were built. On the west end there was a belvedere with other beautiful small shelters on either side of it and a pool of water. Fruit trees, beds of flowers, and aromatic shrubs were planted there. The sultan who took pleasure in planting trees also liked to see beds of flowers. He went there every day not only because this is where his councils were held but because he liked to walk there.

Let us read the account of Trevisano, the doge of Venice's ambassador: "It is a square which stretches out at the foot of the walls and in which very fine equestrian exercises take place. This very big square is twice the size of Saint Mark's and it is longer than it is wide. The sultan's garden is as vast as the square. In the middle of it, one step up from the ground, rises an open kiosk supported by columns and covered with green plants. Cloths are hung on the side and in the back as protection against the heat of the sun, and on each column was hung a cage in which was a small, singing bird. The garden was full of pomegranate trees, pear trees, fig trees, vines, myrtles, and other types of trees."

In May, 1509, the sultan held a celebration in the hippodrome. He had a large, round tent set up and had the pool filled with Nile water brought through the aqueduct, and then he had all the flowers of Cairo gathered up and placed in the pool. All the Koran readers and the preachers were invited. Candelabra were put up, and magnificent rugs were hung around the pool. The sultan invited the four cadis, all the generals and other high-ranking officers, the civil officials, and all the important people. There was a tremendous feast; the meal was served in four hundred porcelain plates from China. Marzipan cakes were prepared. There was a great number of geese, chickens, and sheep. In all, fifteen hundred pounds of meat, one thousand chickens, five hundred geese, fifty fat sheep, and forty lambs were prepared. The cost of this banquet, if pastry, fruit, and sugar are included, was estimated at more than one thousand dinars.

On April 10, 1510, at the time of the Moslem New Year, the sultan appeared at the hippodrome to receive the good wishes of his high-ranking officers. He gave each one of them a rose. The historian who reports this adds: "It is the first time that officers were seen kissing the ground in front of the sultan because they had received a rose."

In 1511 the bushes planted by the sultan in the hippodrome began to grow and bear the most varied and the most marvelous blooms, such as roses, jasmines, irises, lilies, and other rare flowers. Ibn Iyas wrote: "I have seen there a white rose imported from Syria; it has a very sweet smell and is of a species different from the other roses of Egypt. It flowers in the summer at the time when the Nile is at its highest. It was a foreign species that was not found in Egypt. The platform which the sultan ordered set up was inlaid with ivory and ebony and had on it a fluffy, leather-covered cushion. This was where he sat in state, protected by a jasmine bush and servants who kept him cool by waving fans. In the trees hung cages in which were songbirds, such as nightingales with their thousand melodious songs, pigeons with collars, blackbirds, turtledoves, ring-doves, and many other songbirds, while a great variety of other winged creatures flew about in liberty; Abyssinian chickens, Chinese ducks, partridges. The sultan sometimes sat at the edge of the pool, which was forty cubits long and was filled daily with Nile water brought in by the elevating machines of the aqueduct which functioned day and night. A throne was set up for him on this spot almost every Friday, and only the officers that he had designated were admitted in his presence."

This was where the sultan gave magnificent parties for ambassadors who were passing through the country. At the beginning of the sixteenth century various sovereigns often sent missions to the monarch of Egypt. Historians point out that in 1512 there were no less than fourteen ambassadors present at the same time in Cairo. They had been sent by the Sefevid sultan, the king of Georgia, the Ramadanid prince of Cilicia, the Ottoman sultan, the lord of the Turkomans of the White Sheep, the prince of Tunis, the sherif of Mecca, the prince of Bengal, another Turkoman lord, the governor of the province of Aleppo, the commander of the Egyptian expeditionary force in India, the king of France, the doge of Venice, and the Dhoulqadirid prince of Silicia.

# 11

## Epilogue

THE REGIME of the Mamlūk sultans really ended on what
could be called the execution square, the southern gate of
Fatimid Cairo, Bāb Zuweila.

On April 14, 1517, the former sultan Ṭūman Bey, dressed
in a long-sleeved cloak and a skullcap, wearing chains, and
seated on a camel, crossed the city from north to south. At
the Zuweila gate he was made to get off his mount, he was
untied, and he was surrounded by Ottoman soldiers who
carried bared sabers. As soon as he realized that he was
going to be hanged, he stood up before the gate and cried,
"Recite the Fatiha for me three times!" He held out his hand
and recited the prayer himself three times. Then turning
toward the executioner, he said, "Do your work!" A noose
was placed around his neck, and his body was pulled up.
The rope tore and Ṭūman Bey fell to the foot of the gate.
It is even said that the rope gave way twice, dropping the
condemned man to the ground. Finally he was hanged bareheaded, with his body dressed in red rags; his feet were
bound with strips of blue cloth. When he died, a great cry
rose up from the saddened and dismayed crowd.

This execution was to be expected, but unfortunately
Sultan Selim did not stop there. Several months later he was
present at a shadow-theater performance on the island of
Roḍah. The artist showed Zuweila gate and Ṭūman Bey,
represented by a doll, at the time of the hanging. The Ottoman sultan found it very amusing when the rope broke

twice. He gave the artist two hundred dinars and said, "When we leave for Stamboul, come with us so that my son can see this show!"

---

## HISTORICAL TABLE IN SUMMARY

| | |
|---|---|
| Caliphate governors | 640–868 |
| Ṭūlūnids | 868–905 |
| Resumption of the governors' administration | 905–39 |
| Ikhshidids | 939–69 |
| Fatimids | 969–1172 |
| Ayyūbids | 1172–1250 |
| Mamlūk sultans | 1250–1517 |
| Ottoman conquest of Egypt | 1517 |

# Selected Bibliography

Abd al-Laṭīf. *Relation de l'Egypte.* Translated by Silvestre de Sacy. Paris, Imprimerie Royale, 1810.

Affagart, Geffin. *Relation de Terre Sainte.* Edited by J. Chavanon. Paris, V. Lecoffre, 1902.

Anglure, Ogier d'. *Le saint voyage de Jérusalem.* Edited by François Bonnardot and Auguste Longnon. Paris, Firmin-Didot, 1878.

Baumgarten, Martin von. *Peregrinatio in Egyptum.* Nuremberg, 1594.

Belon, Pierre. *Les observations en Grèce, Asie, Egypte, Arabie.* Paris, 1555.

Breydenbach, Bernhard von. *Les saintes pérégrinations.* Text and translation annotated by F. Larrivaz. Cairo, 1904.

Casanova, Paul. "Histoire et description de la Citadelle du Caire." *Mémoires de la Mission archéologique française du Caire.* Tome VI. Cairo, 1897.

Clerget, Marcel. *Le Caire.* Cairo, E. and R. Schindler, 1934.

Dopp, P. H. "Le Caire vu par les voyageurs occidentaux du moyen âge." *Bulletin de la Société royale de géographie d'Egypte.* Tome XXIII, 117–49; Tome XXIV, 115–62. Cairo, 1950–51.

Franz, Julius. *Kairo.* Leipzig, E. A. Seemann, 1903.

Hautecoeur, Louis, and Gaston Wiet. *Les mosquées du Caire.* Paris, Ernest Leroux, 1932.

Ibn Baṭṭūṭah. *Voyages.* Translated by C. Defrèmery and B. R. Sanguinetti. Paris, 1853–58.

Ibn Iyas. *Histoire des Mamlouks Circassiens*. Translated by Gaston Wiet. Cairo, 1945.

——. *Journal d'un bourgeois du Caire*. Translated by Gaston Wiet. Paris, A. Colin, 1955–60.

Ibn Jubayr. *Voyages*. Translated by Maurice Gaudefroy-Demombynes. Paris, G. Geuthner, 1950–60.

Ibn Khaldūn. *Prolégomènes*. Translated by W. MacGuckin de Slane. Paris, 1856–68.

Idrīsi. *Description de l'Afrique et de l'Espagne*. Translated by R. Dozy and M. J. de Goeje. Leyden, E. J. Brill, 1864–66.

Lane, Edward William. *An Account of the Manners and Customs of the Modern Egyptians*. 2 vols. London, 1836–37.

Lane-Poole, Stanley. *Cairo: History, Monuments, Social Life*. London, J. S. Virtue and Co., 1892.

——. *A History of Egypt in the Middle Ages*. London, Methuen and Co., 1901.

——. *Saladin and the Fall of the Kingdom of Jerusalem*. London, 1898.

——. *The Story of Cairo*. London, J. M. Dent and Co., 1902.

Leo Africanus. *Description de l'Afrique*. Translated and edited by A. Epaulard. Paris, A. Maisonneuve, 1956.

Maqrīzi. "Description topographique et historique de l'Egypte." Translated by Paul Casanova. *Mémoires de l'Institut français d'archéologie orientale*. Tomes III–IV. Cairo, 1906–20.

Margoliouth, David Samuel. *Cairo, Jerusalem, and Damascus*. London, 1917.

Migeon, Gaston. *Le Caire*. Paris, H. Laurens, 1906.

Naṣir-i-Khūsrau. *Sefer Nameh*. Translated and edited by Charles Schefer. Paris, 1881.

Piloti, Emmanuel. *L'Egypte au commencement du quinzième siècle*. Edited by P. H. Dopp. Cairo, 1950.

Ravaisse, P. "Essai sur l'histoire et la topographie du Caire." *Mémoires de la Mission archéologique française du Caire.* Tomes I, III. Cairo, 1886–89.

Rhoné, Arthur. *L'Egypte à petites journées*. Paris, Société générale d'éditions, 1910.

Salmon, Georges. "Etudes sur la topographie du Caire." *Mémoires de l'Institut français d'archéologie orientale.* Tome VII. Cairo, 1902.

Sladen, Douglas B. W. *Oriental Cairo*. London, 1911.

Thenaud, Jean. *Le voyage d'Outremer*. Edited by Charles Schefer. Paris, Ernest Leroux, 1884.

Wiet, Gaston. *L'Egypte arabe. Histoire de la nation égyptienne*. Directed by Gabriel Hanotaux. Tome IV. Paris, 1937.

# Index

## CITY OF ART AND COMMERCE

CAIRO, because it was to Egypt of the Middle Ages what other cities of the Nile Valley had been in the ancient past, richly merits its place as the sixteenth city chosen for THE CENTERS OF CIVILIZATION SERIES. For historians, it is perhaps the Islamic center which has excited most interest. Its position in the history of art derives from the brilliant flourishing of architectural works which survive in many sections of the modern city. From the northern walls of the Fatimid town to the powerful Mosque of Sultan Hasan, the stones still sing the glory of the past.

Great Cairo, as European travelers have called it, was a political capital from its very creation. As the center of Shī'ism, the city was detested, and there was an attempt to limit its influence by a type of sanitary cordon. The city, moreover, had rivals at that time, even though they were only, at one pole, Baghdad, the old center of Islam which had replaced Damascus, and, at the other, Cordova, the center of an unexcelled civilization. Under the sultans of the Mamlūk dynasty Cairo ranked as a universal metropolis, while remaining an

*(Continued on back flap)*